Ya Mon, Me Hear Jamaica Talkin'

By Rev. Dr. D. L. Zimmermann

PublishAmerica

Baltimore

First printing

PublishAmerica has allowed this work to remain exactly as the author intended, verbatim, without editorial input.

Hardcover 978-1-4489-3253-5
Softcover 978-1-4489-5589-3
PUBLISHED BY PUBLISHAMERICA, LLLP
www.publishamerica.com
Baltimore

Printed in the United States of America

Foreword

By John Torres, Senior Pastor Goodwill Church Montgomery NY

"Diane Zimmermann is a great blessing to our congregation on many levels. I'm grateful that her books on Jamaica and the Proverbs are soon to be published and made widely available. She has a passion for Christ and His people that elevates the spiritual temperature in any room she enters. Her heart for service to God and for wounded people to receive healing in Christ is unmatched. Let her enthusiasm for missions and Scripture inspire you."

I dedicate this book to my God, Lord and Savior Jesus Christ, whom through Him all things are possible.

I give honor to my parents Joseph and Gloria Percoco who brought me up in the way I should go. The love and support of my sister Gloria and brother Joseph, and to my children Jonathan, Jeremy and Jessica Mandia whom are my blessings on this earth.

My husband Rennie and my friends have assisted me with this book and I am very grateful.

Philippians 4:14
I can do all things through Christ which strengtheneth me.

Table of Contents

The Jamaican Culture and Storytelling

In Jamaica as well as other countries around the world everyone loves a good story. As a small child I would listened intently as my parents and grandparents read me books and told me bed time stories about my guardian Angels, heaven about Jesus and said our prayers. My grandmother would always tell me to" watch out for the "wolf"! I always thought it was the wolf in the fable of the Three Little Pigs. Later on in life I found it to be a parable and nothing to do with a real wolf.

My grandmother Ermanna Gilda who was born in 1891 in Piedmont Italy, was full of stories about our ancestors and the life they had on their farm on the Italian Alps, her father and mother and the impact that Napoleon had on their society. It was a mixture of history, oral tradition and family. My dad would tell us whimsical bedtime's stories about "Mr. Whiskers" who was no bigger than his thumb who rode the back of a butterfly doing good for the creatures of the forest. I had great pool of knowledge to pool from when it came time for me to take my place in telling stories as a Story Teller!

Storytelling is a very significant element in most cultures and seem to link us back to the past though our imagination to the part of the world where our families originated from, in my case Northern European. The same is true for the storytelling in the Jamaican culture because it links them back to their African roots from West Africa.

My family had a traveling "American Indian Village" that toured the United States and Canada in the 1960 bringing the Culture, Art and traditions of the Native Americans. I learned many Native American stories included drumming, dance and singing and all had animal or spiritual relationships that also seem to parallel the Jamaican Anasi stories.

By telling stories, storytellers preserve Jamaican folklores for many generations, ensuring that their culture and African slaves brought to the island of Jamaica their culture through storytelling and preserved their folklores for generations to come and keeping their history alive. Jamaican proverbs allowed slaves to communicate with one another without their masters understanding what they were saying.

Folk legends are also part of Jamaica's storytelling history. The Jamaica Insider says that some well-known folk legends include "Brear Anansi" or "brother Spider." The story is about trickery and deceit and about naughty "big bwoy." Jamaican parents tell their children these stories to stir fear in their hearts. Many Jamaican adults recall being paralyzed with fear after hearing stories of a "duppy."(spirits)

In additions to folk legends, proverbs and fables are integral to Jamaica's storytelling legacy. Although they no longer have to deceive slave masters, these proverbs are still used by modern-day Jamaicans as local idioms. Jamaica Insider says "they are used as a short and quick way of conveying certain thoughts and feelings without using their long and elaborate English versions."

Interestingly, Jamaica is a melting pot in the Caribbean with cultures as diverse as Africans, Europeans, East Indians, Chinese, Arabs, Jews, and Persians. There are no indigenous people on the island; all of them are imports from somewhere else. Even though all of them have had some influence in the country, African heritage seems to dominate the region.

All groups on the island have adopted the stories of Africa and made them a part of themselves. They live by their nation's motto, "Out of Many, One People." This statement exemplifies Jamaica's feelings about their cultural diversity.

Storytelling and Oral Tradition

The oral tradition of storytelling was the only way information was passed down from generation to generation. In remote places of the world storytelling is still the only way to communicate and hand down their cultural values and history.

The "Animal" stories in the Caribbean have links to African-American tales of the Uncle Remus tradition, who in turn have direct links to Africa, especially the West African Gold Coast of Ghana and the Ashanti people—the birthplace of "Anancy the Spider." The Characters Found in Anasi Stories.

Throughout the Caribbean, Anancy the spider is also known as Brer 'Nancy, is a very popular character. He is wise, cunning, greedy, lazy and full of tricks, and he rules supreme over the other animals. Anancy is both the hero and the villain, both loveable and sinister, and is known to have magical powers and lives by his wits.

As a trickster, the main character often deceives and exploits his fellow creatures for his own benefit. "Tricksters will themselves be duped and humbled. And however selfish and course they are, their antics provoke affectionate laughter, while their quick wits and mystic power inspire awe."

Among the Ashanti people he is known as "Ananci Krokoko," translated as "The Great Spider," and is a symbol of wisdom. In the world of storytelling, all the animals and insects have the power of speech. They dress like humans, live like humans and think like humans. They are very much a reflection of us and often show our human weaknesses, stupidity, greed and ignorance. That is why we can relate to them and often see people or ourselves as the hero, villain or trickster in the stories. There are numerous characters in the form of the Goat, Rabbit, Tiger, Monkey, Dog, Snake and Donkey, to name a few.

The American Mix and Animal Folktales

In America, the main characters of the "Uncle Remus" tales written by Joel Chandler Harris are the Rabbit and the Fox known as Brer Rabbit and Brer Fox. The "Brer" is an early African-American abbreviation for "Brother."

As you might know by Walt Disney's production of Uncle Remus, he was an old Negro slave who held the full attention of the seven year-old son of his master when he relays the tales and stories of Brer Rabbit, Brer Fox and a host of other characters. Many of these stories have parallels all over Europe, the Old and the New World cultures of the African slaves, the American Indians and the Europeans were well mixed and over time they took from each other, put in their own cultural twists, dialect and nuances and retold the tales.

The author Joel Chandler Harris (1848-1908) is famous for his creation of Uncle Remus, Brer Rabbit, Brer Fox, Brer Bear and other characters as in: Uncle Remus, His Songs and His Sayings (1880), Nights with Uncle Remus (1883), Uncle Remus and His Friends (1892), The Tar Baby (1904), Uncle Remus and Brer Rabbit (1906); edited Uncle Remus's Magazine (1907-08). Other works included Mingo, and Other Sketches in Black and White (1884), Free Joe and Other Georgia Sketches (1887), Gabriel Tolliver (1902).

Joel Chandler Harris grew up in Georgia during the Civil War and spent his lifetime compiling and publishing the tales told to him by former slaves. Many of these stories Joel Chandler Harris learned from an old black man he called "Uncle George" and these were first published as columns in "The Atlanta Constitution" and were later syndicated nationwide and published in book form. Harris's Uncle Remus was a fictitious old slave and philosopher who told entertaining fables about Br'er Rabbit and other woodland creatures in a Southern black dialect.

Jamaican Patois Dialect in Telling Stories

If you are not use to hearing Patois spoken you will not know what they are saying right away, even though it is English. That is how I came to write this book. As I ministered in a local church in the mountains of Upstate New York, a majority of the congregation membership of my church were from Jamaica, WI. Mostly they arrive in our community as migrant laborers who worked on the apple farms during the seasons and then would return, and others settled here to live and bring their wives and children. After services I would take the words I didn't understand and use my Learn to Speak Jamaican translator to understand the stories and phrases they would say to me. As time went by I understood better the Jamaican terminology.

Many times I didn't understand without a full explanation. For example the word "packney" was the world for children, and every question was spoken and answered with a proverb or a parable.

One song we sang in church on Sunday morning was:
Fi mi, fi mi, fi me, Jesus a fi mi! Fa you, fa you, fa you, Jesus a fa you!

which translates:

For me, for me, for me, Jesus is for me! For you, for you, Jesus is for you!
I loved the song and the reggae type beat.

For my Jamaican friends they would not give up speaking their dialect. The thicker the dialect is better when speaking around me because they knew I didn't understand and they would find it amusing. My church sisters Maybel Stewart and Lovena Burrowes from Jamaica would take the time to speak slower and explain what they meant so I would understand.

God is good all the time and I know that dialect plays an important part in telling a story which makes the situation with the characters real and funny. It also gives the story color and life, but for persons whose ears are not used to hearing the unique sounds and pronunciations of a particular dialect, the stories could be confusing and difficult to understand, but for the local population of Caribbean islanders, the stronger the dialect the funnier the story.

In Jamaica, stories are told in the local "Patois". The following is an excerpt from the story by Louise Bennett, written in patois with a Standard English translation after.

Anancy talking to Tiger:
"Lawd, Bra Tigar, me hooda glad fi goh wid yuh, but afta me soh sick, me disha dead wid me belly an me cyaan walk a tall."

("Lord, Brother Tiger, I would have been glad to go with you, but I am so sick, I feel like I'm going to die with this stomachache and I cannot walk at all.")

The African Connection to Jamaican Folklore

Folktales about Anancy or other spellings: Anancy, Anance, Anansi ('Nansi) or even Brer Nansi. has its roots in the Ashanti folktales which are about the trickster Anancy, the spider-man, as the hare is the chief character in the Yoruba folktales and the tortoise in the stories of the Ibo people. Songs often accompany the stories and have inspired many Jamaican folksongs.

Anancy the Spiderman was brought from the west coast of Africa by the first slaves and went and Jamaicans added innumerable prodigy - Brer Tacoma, Brer Tiger and others to the Anancy folktales.

Anancy is quick-witted and intelligent surviving the odds and tricking those around him. He personifies the quality of survival so admired by Jamaicans. You may see his name spelled in a variety of ways; Bra 'Nansi filled the role of storyteller hero or villain. He was great at disguises, omniscient but nonetheless willing to be chopped to prove a moral. He was something to everyone: his indestructibility, knowledge and wit were an investment in hope.

Mostly Anancy stories are satirical and cynical and they never have a live-happily-ever-after ending like most European bedtime stories have. 'Nansi stories are told to children at bedtime, with the storyteller making them up as they go along. The Anancy stories belong to "evening time."

As in the West African stories Anancyi is "craven" (greedy) and, being small and weak, he wins by guile not by strength. Anancy is an indestructible and irresistible spider who is both, "fooler and fool, maker and unmade, wily and stupid, subtle and gross, the High Gods accomplice and his rival."

The Characters in Anasi Stories

Louise Bennett, author states that Anancy takes many shapes; at times, he seems to be a man, and at other times, he is an insect, running his web and taking refuge in the ceiling. Anancy Stories are filled with animal characters and their characteristics are so human like that you begin to feel as though the characters are the same people who are part of your lives and history. The effect of these stories on children was not only morally fulfilling, but pure enjoyment as well.

In the collection of Anansi stories by Louise Bennett - Anancy* and Miss Lou, Sangster's Book Stores Jamaica - few of the characters are human. Humans are usually kings, and their daughters, the princesses, who greedy Anansi is usually anxious to marry, mainly for their legacy.

The other characters cover a wide range of insects and animals - mosquito, wasp, rat, cat, dog, snake, cow, goat, mongoose, monkey, donkey, lion, and tiger. Anansi tricks many of these animals out of their good fortune, or is the direct cause of some peculiar trait which they possess; e.g. is Anansi why hog mouth long; why rat live in a hole; why fowl eat roach, and so on. In one story, fire becomes a character. When Anansi first sees her, she is a pretty little dancing girl.

He invites her home and as she travels along the path of dry twigs that he has laid down to lead her to his house, she becomes larger and larger and turns into a large 'outa size' woman, which burns down his house. According to the story it is this flirtation with Fire which causes houses to be burnt ever since.

The stories are male dominated; usually the characters are introduced as Bredda this or that - Bredda Rat, Bredda Tiger and so on. Females are represented mostly by the princesses, and of course, Anansi's wife. He is not always married, however. In many stories he is free to go courting as it pleases him.

Most of the characters have their generic names, so we know exactly who they are. One puzzling character, however, is the one named Tacooma or Tucumah or Tacoma or Tookooma - like many stories out of the oral tradition, the spelling varies in the written form. Tacooma is an interesting character; he is often stronger and braver than Anansi and is the only character which Anansi can't always outwit.

In "Anancy is Riding Horse' in Folklore from Contemporary Jamaicans by Daryl Dance, we get this account: "- the same Tacuma -Anancy is always a stupid, an im always mek Tacoma turn him fool." According to the experts Anansi stories came with the slaves from the Gold Coast. In Twi Ananse means spider (their spider god) and nkituma, his son has become the Tacooma in the Jamaican Anansi stories.

Daryl Dance identifies Tacooma as "A frequent character in Anancy tales. (Sometimes) Tacuma is Anancy's companion, sometimes his son, sometimes his spouse, sometimes his neighbour". This multiplicity of characterization, it seems to me makes Tacooma even more wily and 'trickify' than Anansi.

An African Tale: How Anansi Came to Own All the Tales of the World

In the beginning, Nyame the Sky God owned all the stories told in the world. Anansi the spider wanted to own the stories, since everywhere he looked, there were tales. So he went to Nyame, and asked if he could buy the stories from him.

Now, Anansi was not the first person to ask Nyame for the right to tell the stories. Many great and powerful families had petitioned the god, and he had named a price that none had been able to meet. "There are three things which I want in exchange for the stories," Nyame said. "No one has been able to bring them to me before."

"I shall have better luck," Anansi promised. "What are these things?"

"I want Mmoboro, Onini, and Osebo: the hornets, the python, and the leopard."

"Very well," Anansi said. "I shall bring them to you."

So Anansi went home. He found a gourd, and made a hole in it. Then he set off for the hornets' tree. He stopped at the river and splashed himself with water, and then carried more water to the tree and splashed it on the hornets.

"Can't you see that it's raining?" he called to the hornets. "Why don't you foolish people go someplace dry?"

"Where should we go?" they buzzed.

"This gourd is dry," Anansi said, and when all the hornets had flown inside, he plugged the hole.

"Foolish people," he said, and brought the hornets to Nyame.

Next, Anansi cut a bamboo pole and carried it to Onini's house. When he grew close, he began muttering to himself. "Stupid woman, stupid woman."

The python heard Anansi, and came outside. "Why are you talking to yourself?"

"My wife and I had an argument," Anansi sighed. "She says that you are shorter and weaker than this bamboo pole; I say that you must be longer and stronger."

"Well, it is a question that is easily answered," Onini replied. "Bring the pole here."

So Onini stretched out beside the pole. "Stretch more," Anansi said, and Onini complied. "No, wait, you are slipping," Anansi said. "Let me tie you to the pole, so that we know the measurement is accurate." And when he had tied Onini's head to the pole, he ran to the other end and tied his tail, and wrapped a vine about him.

"It appears that I was wrong," Anansi said to his captive. "You are shorter and weaker than this pole, and very foolish besides." And he carried Onini to Nyame.

Anansi went to the forest where he knew Osebo walked. He dug a pit, and covered it so that even he could barely tell where it was. That night, as Osebo prowled about, he stepped into Anansi's trap and fell. In the morning, Anansi peered over the edge of the pit. "Unfortunate creature!" he said.

"I cannot get out of this trap," the leopard said. "Please help me."

"Well, I am certainly very sorry for you," Anansi answered. "But if I helped you out, I'm sure that you would forget my kindness, and as soon as you grew hungry you would try to eat me and my family."

"I swear that will not happen," Osebo said.

"Very well, then, I believe you." Anansi picked up a rope, and bent a tree down over the pit and tied it in place. He tied a second rope to the top of the tree and threw the other end into the pit.

"Tie this to your tail," he instructed.

"It is done," the leopard said after a moment.

"In that case, you are a very foolish creature," Anansi said, and cut the rope which held the tree down. The tree snapped back into place, pulling Osebo after it. He hung upside down, twisting helplessly, and Anansi killed him and brought his body to Nyame.

The sky god was impressed. "You have met my conditions. Henceforth, all stories belong to you, and the tellers of tales must acknowledge you as the owner."

And that is how, by using cleverness instead of strength and riches, Anansi the spider became the owner of all tales that are told.

West African Tale:
Anansi Claims His Fame

Everyone knows Anansi the spider craves attention. He plays his tricks on others because he likes to win. One day as he walked through the jungle, he noticed how important Tiger was. Tiger was king of the jungle, and that was why the lilies were called tiger lilies, and the beetles were called tiger beetles, and many moths were known as tiger moths, and even some of the stones looked like, and were called, tiger's eyes.

Anansi decided he had to have something named after him, and he began to skitter around the forest on his eight legs, calling out, "I'm Anansi, and I'm as strong and brave as Tiger. I want something named after ME." Now Tiger overheard Anansi's boastful cries. He yawned and rolled over and chuckled to himself. He looked up at Anansi and said, "You? You're a tiny little thing. Why would anything be named after you?"

"I'm important," Anansi said. "I'm brave. I can do anything." Again Tiger laughed. "Anything? Well, then, capture Snake and bring him to me, and if you do that, we'll give something your name." "I want our stories named after me," Anansi said.

Again Tiger laughed. "If you capture Snake, I promise we'll call our stories 'Anansi stories.'" Anansi was thrilled, and he ran off to capture Snake. Tiger yawned and rolled over again, for he knew nobody could capture Snake. He was a wily and slippery fellow. Anansi didn't have a chance. But Anansi thought hard, and decided that the best way to catch Snake was to trap him in a vine. He cut a strong vine and tied a loop at one end, and placed the loop in the thick grass right beside Snake's path. Then he put some ripe fruit in the center of the loop, held the other end of the vine and hid in the bush. Before long Snake slithered along the path. Naturally when he saw the fruit, he slipped across the vine to eat it. Anansi tugged on that vine, but when Snake felt the vine slipping around his slinky body, he quickly slipped away.

Anansi was troubled, but just a little bit. He went home to think. "A trap will never work," he said to himself. "Snake can climb trees and slither and slide away, so I'll have to outsmart him. And I'm the smartest fellow there is!" The next day Anansi woke with a new plan. He cut a long bamboo pole, and this he lay across Snake's path. Then he began to pace up and down along the pole, muttering to himself. Snake watched from the grass until his curiosity overcame him. "What on earth are you doing, Anansi?" Snake hissed from his hiding place.

Anansi grinned and pointed at his pole. "I have cut a bamboo pole!" he said proudly. "What of it?" Snake asked. "Who cares about a bamboo pole?" "Ah," said Anansi, "but this is a long bamboo pole. This bamboo pole is longer than you." Snake flicked his tongue. "It is not," he said. "And I'll prove it." He slithered to the pole and stretched himself along its length. "There, you see, Anansi. I'm much longer than your pole."

Anansi shook his head. "You're not," he said. "You can see your tail is shorter." "It's not!" cried Snake, and he stretched himself out. "Ah," said Anansi, "but I know your tricks. When I stand at the end, you ease your head back at the other end. You're cheating, Snake. My pole is much longer than you." "I never cheat," Snake said.

"You are," Anansi said, running to the head of the pole. There lay Snake's head. "You see, your head may be level with this end of the pole, but I'm sure your tail no longer reaches the far end." "It does," Snake said, and Anansi ran to the other end of the pole, and sure enough Snake's tail was even. "But there, you see," Anansi said, "you've eased your head down." On and on they argued in this way until Anansi said: "I know the solution. I'll tie your tail to this end so you cannot slither up. Then I'll know you're not cheating."

"Go ahead," Snake said confidently. Anansi tied Snake's tail to the pole and ran to the other end. Sure enough, there was Snake's head, reaching beyond the pole. "You're still cheating," Anansi said angrily. "How can I measure fairly when you keep easing your head forward? You won't stay still!" "I'm still!" Snake said. "Go on, tie my head to the pole." And so Anansi did. "There, you see!" Snake said. "You're wriggling up and down. I'm sure that my pole is longer."

"Tie my middle then, and you'll see," Snake hissed. And so Anansi tied Snake's middle to the pole, and as soon as the knot was tight, he lifted the pole over his shoulder, with Snake securely tied to it. He set off at once to find Tiger. "Here he is!" Anansi cried. Tiger was amazed. "You outwitted Snake," Tiger said while Snake sniffled and snuffled. "Set me free," he cried. "But remember your promise, Tiger," Anansi said. Tiger remembered, and ever since that day, all the stories have been called Anansi stories, and Snake has never let anyone try to measure him again.

Anansi and the Snake

Anansi stepped off the ship and took off his hat and held it in his hands. "Where's the party?" he shouted. Then he listened for the sound of calypso and regge music. What he heard was silence. Anansi sniffed the air and licked his lips expecting to smell aromas of tropical foods in the air. But no foods were cooking.

"Where's the party, mon?" shouted Anansi. "Where are the bright colors? Where are the happy people? I brought my party hat and want to eat and sing and dance." He had been to this island in the Caribbean many times before and always had a good time. Now the island was quiet. The people were dressed in dark clothing. No singing or music could be heard. No smells of food were in the air,

Usually the people loved to see Anansi. He sometimes was called Anansi the Spider - when he chose to appear in the form of a spider, and sometimes just called Anansi when he appeared as a man. He was known for his quick wit and his fun stories. Right now, the people were pressing their fingers to their lips and telling him to shhhh. Spider or man, they wanted him quiet!

"What's wrong with everyone?" asked Anansi. "I came to party, and you all keep telling me to 'Shhhh'."

"It's the snake," one islander finally whispered as he looked with fear towards the Jungle. "In the middle of the jungle lives a giant Snake, a python! It is larger than any Snake we have ever seen. It ate most of the jungle animals. It also ate most of our cows and the pigs." (This explains why there were so few cows and pigs on that Caribbean island) "The python also eats any people who come to close to where he lives by the river."

"If we cook our island foods, the snake smells it and comes to eat. If we play music or sing and play Calypso and Reggae, the Snake hears and comes to the party. If we dress in our bright clothes, he sees us and comes to us. We are afraid. There will be no parties on the island until the Snake is gone!" This said, the man looked around.

Anansi looked around also and saw everyone's head bobbing up and down sadly. "Where is this snake?" shouted Anansi. "I will kill the Snake!"

"Oh, no!" whispered another. We already called upon the sky God to save us from the snake." He told us to use our wits, but that we could not kill the python.

"I made python," said the sky God. "I can't unmake him. Nor will I kill him, but if anyone can stop him from his murderous ways, I will reward them with a present."

"If we kill the Snake, said the people, the sky god will send the 'hurricane' to blow across our island." "The villagers threw up their hands."Who is clever enough to destroy the Snake?" They asked. "Who is brave enough or stupid enough to try."

This was when Anansi the Spider realized the Sky God had promised a PRESENT for stopping the snake from killing. Any present from the sky god would be an outrageously fantastic present. Besides, the Snake was keeping him from having a party on the island.

Anansi told the villagers to get him a bowl filed with warm fresh bread, fresh fruit and large chicken eggs and a long rope. Then he told them to cut down a tall tree and strip off the branches and carry it down by the river. The villagers worked very fast because they didn't want to be near the river if the Snake came out of its hole. But the giant Python lay sleeping while Anansi crawled up by the hole and started a conversation with no one to listen to him except himself and the Snake. "No, no!"He said out loud to himself. "You are wrong about the snake," Anansi loudly shouted. He is nice. He won't hurt me. Especially when he sees the presents I have brought to him."

Then Anansi quickly walked to the other side of the hole and pretended to be a villager once more! "But the snake is EVIL! He eats our cows and people and scares us to death."

Anansi moved back quietly to the first side of the hole again and said, "I won't let you talk about the snake that way. Take that" - and he hit a stick on the ground and yelled in pain. "Take that you liar!" and Anansi slapped a stick noisily on the mud before continuing.

"Even if the Snake eats things, he is the biggest snake in the world, and I want to meet him. You go away!" All these praises about the Python kept flowing from Anansi's mouth until the Snake came out of his hole.

But, the only one he saw was Anansi. This was no surprise to the snake - for snakes cannot see very far and hunt their food by smell and by the vibrations their prey makes when it moves. Anansi said to the snake, "I taught that villager a lesson - He ran off! He will not insult you again!" Anansi then held out the loaves of warm bread

Thinking the loaves were Anansi's arms, the python flicked its tongue and touched them to taste them. The snake's head came out of the hole more, and Anansi let go of the loaves just as the snake grabbed them with his fangs. Then, Anansi rolled the fruit farther out past the entrance to the hole. Feeling the vibrations - the snake came out further yet and swallowed up the fruit. Then Anansi presented python with the eggs. Now everyone knows that snakes like to eat eggs. And the snake unhinged his jaws and swallowed the eggs - bowl and all.

Then the Snake looked at Anansi and thought…dessert!

"I am honored to meet you face to face," said Anansi. He was less afraid since he knew the Snake had already eaten something and was less hungry than before.

"Most creatures do not live long after they are so honored," hissed the Snake. "But you seem different than the others and more intelligent."

"Oh yes," said brother Anansi, "The people of this island are not very bright. They say you are not the longest snake in the world. They say you are only long enough to coil around a cow."

"What?" Hissed the snake. "Not long?"
"But," continued Anansi, "I tell them you are long enough to coil around a house or a village." Then Anansi paused, "Exactly how long are you, Mr. Snake? I can't see your whole body."

Python came farther out of his hole. He was huge, but Anansi hid his fear. "You are huge - but come out so I can measure you and prove you are the biggest snake in the world."

Python crawled out of his hole inch after inch and foot after foot.

"Can you see this log?" asked Anansi, patting his hand on the bare wood. If you lie down beside it I can measure you."

Well, the snake didn't like people saying he was smaller than someone else, so he slithered over next to the log.

"Now," Anansi said - "If I tie a piece of rope around you every ten paces - I can count up the ropes and see how long you are and prove you are the biggest Snake in the world." This sounded reasonable to the Python, and he let Anansi begin to tie his tail to the log.

"Say," said python after turning his head and staring straight into Anansi's eyes, "Your knots are really tight."

"I can loosen them if you wish," said Anansi, "if you don't want to stretch to your longest and prove you are truly the longest Snake in the world."

"Oh, no!" said Python. "Make them tighter yet! But hurry up. This is uncomfortable." Then Python closed his eyes thinking about how delicious Anansi would be to eat when he was done!

Anansi finished tying the snake to the log. Then he asked, "Can you move and stretch further?"

"I can't move at all," said the snake.

"That's what I've been waiting!" for shouted Anansi. IT'S PARTY TIME!!! Then he put on his party hat and began dancing around.

"Truly you might be the biggest Snake in the world, but your brain is small. I have you tied up and you can't eat any more cows on this island. And you certainly won't eat any more people." Then since he knew Sky God didn't want Python killed, he pushed the log that held the snake right into the Caribbean Sea where he floated to South America.

"Sky God, Did you see that?" asked Anansi. I put a stop to the Snake's evil ways without killing him. That's when Sky God gave Anansi a present. He gave him a small box with enough wisdom and cleverness for a lifetime. This cleverness made Anansi famous throughout the world.

The people put on their brightly colored clothing. They cooked their finest meals and let the smoke fill the air with magnificent scents. They sang and played Calypso and Regge music and told wonderful stories. If you go to the Caribbean today, you may still hear some of the wonderful stories about Anansi and the Python.

And the Python? ...He still lives in the rainforests of South America. And some people today are still trying to find him so they can say they have measured the longest snake in the world.

Why Dogs Watch People Eat—
An Anansi Tale

Those who have heard Anansi stories before already know that Anansi sometimes appears as a man and sometimes takes the form of a spider. So it makes sense that Anansi and Dog were once good friends. After all, Dog is often called "man's best friend." The two often traveled together and shared everything as they traveled. But one day they both decided to separate to look for good pieces of land to farm.

Dog found the perfect piece of land. It had good soil that looked like it was fertile. It had water beside it to irrigate crops if the weather was dry. There were few trees to clear and no rocks to dig up. Dog howled in happiness. Then he went to look for Anansi.

When Anansi saw the spot, he fell in love with it too. Even though Dog was his friend, Anansi decided that he should have the land instead of Dog. So he said, "My friend, I remember my father planted yams on this very spot, and they were big!" "How big were they?" asked Dog.

Before Anansi answered, he grabbed a tree branch above his head and changed into a Spider, and hung on the branch from a single strand of webbing. Then Anansi said, "The yams were the size of my legs."Dog looked at Anansi's legs. They were skinny like threads. After all, Anansi was a spider with thin spider sized legs. Who would want to grow yams so thin? "Before I work land that grows yams so small, I would rather walk around and find another piece of land to farm." And that's what he did.

When Dog left, Anansi bought the land. But, instead of skinny yams, Anansi grew the biggest yams that anyone had ever seen. Dog howled and howled when he found out the land he had let go turned out to be the best farm land around.

Whenever Dog saw someone eating one of those yams; he was reminded how Anansi cheated him out of buying the rich land. And Dog still looks to see what everyone is eating. He watches every bite you take. Whenever you eat, your dog is sure to be looking at you if you own one.

Anansi

There are stories of Anansi the Spider that tell how skillful and clever he was. These stories are true. There are also stories about how lazy and deceitful Anansi the Spider could be at times. Unfortunately, these stories are also true.

Anansi was a very skillful farmer. He worked alongside his wife and son for an entire year to clear land to farm. They had worked together before to farm small patches of land. But this was the biggest patch of land they had ever cleared.

They planted the field with yams, maize and beans. The crop was huge, the biggest they had ever grown. Anansi was pleased when he saw all the corn and beans and knew the yams would be just as nice when they were dug up. Suddenly, Anansi's pleasure turned to greed. He did not want to share such wealth with anyone, including his own wife and son.

He called his wife and son when the crops were ripe and ready to harvest and said, "We have all worked hard to prepare these fields and to grow these crops. Let us now harvest the crops and put them into our barn. When that is done, we all will need some rest. You and our son should go home to our village to relax for a few weeks. I must travel far away from home on business. When I return home, we will all come to the farm and enjoy a great feast."

Anansi's wife and son thought this was a good idea and went straight back to the village. This left Anansi to his mischief. He built himself a comfortable hut near the farm and began to feast on the harvest by himself. He slept during the heat of the day and came out at night to gather food and prepare it for himself. There would be no one to share with.

Before very long, Anansi's son began to feel guilty for resting while his father was on a business trip. So he traveled back to the farm to weed between the rows and prepare the fields for the next season. As he worked he passed by the barn and noticed that large amounts of the food they harvested had disappeared. He thought robbers had stolen the harvest.

Anansi's son returned to the village and told the people what had happened. They made a stick figure and covered it with straw to make it look like a man. Then they covered the straw with sticky tar and helped carry the figure out to the field to wait for evening. Some of the men remained with Anansi's son to watch and help him catch the thieves.

Anansi was not aware of what had happened and came out of his hiding place to get more food from the barn. On his way to the barn he saw the figure of a man standing in his field. Anansi raced right over to the figure and said, "This field belongs to my family. Get out of here. When the figure did not move and did not speak, Anansi hit the figure with his right hand.

Anansi's hand was stuck tight to the figure. "How dare you grab my hand? I'll hit you again. Anansi hit the figure with his left hand, which also became stuck in the tar. Anansi tried to push his foot against the middle of the figure to free his hands. The foot became stuck. Then he kicked out with the other foot. Soon Anasi was not even on the ground. He was hanging in the air, stuck to the tar figure in the field. And there he stayed until daybreak.

Anansi's son and the villagers came out of hiding and ran to where they had left the figure in the field. They came with sticks and clubs to punish the robber. They were all quite surprised that the thief was really Anansi. The villagers all laughed except for Anansi's son who was quite ashamed of his greedy father.

Anansi was so embarrassed that he had been so selfish and greedy that he turned into a spider and ran away to hide. He went from one spot to another. Whenever anyone saw Anansi, they laughed at him. This happened time after time until Anansi finally went to hide in the dark, dusty corners of the ceiling where he was not likely to be seen. That's where he can usually be found to this day.

How Anansi Thought He Tricked God

Anansi was terribly conceited after the whole affair of the ear of corn. God found Anansi entertaining, but his bragging was growing tiresome. So God gave Anansi a sack and said, "I have something in mind; figure it out and bring it back to me in the sack." Anansi asked questions, but God would give no further clues as to what that "something" might be.

God sent the mortal on his way, saying that if he were only half as clever as he boasted he was, then he should have no problem figuring out what "something" God wanted. Anansi was puzzled. How was he to know what God wanted in the sack? He left heaven and had a meeting with the birds, explaining his predicament. The birds were sympathetic, but had no clues to offer. However, each agreed to give Anansi one feather, enabling Anansi to fly.

Anansi made these feathers into a beautiful cloak, and then flew up to heaven, where he perched in a tree next to God's house. Some of the people of heaven saw this strange "bird" and began talking about it. They asked each other what kind of bird this might be. God himself did not recall making any sort of creature that looked like that. One of those present suggested that, if Anansi were clever, he might know what sort of bird this was. Anansi, in the tree, heard all of this.

God's attendants were speaking among themselves when one said, "Good luck finding Anansi - God sent him on an impossible mission. How was Anansi to know that God wanted the sun and the moon brought to him in a sack?" Overhearing this, Anansi went out to fetch the sun and the moon.

He went to the python, the wisest of all things, and asked how one might capture the sun and the moon. The python advised him to go to the west, where the sun rests at night. The moon could be found in the east around the same time. So Anansi gathered the sun and the moon, placed them in the sack, and took them to God. God was so pleased with Anansi's ingenuity that he made Anansi his captain on earth.

The Cricket Match and Brother Anancy

Once upon a time, Brother Anancy had a plan to go to the cricket match in town, which was far away. He did not have enough money so he came up with a plan. He went to see Brother Snake and Brother Rabbit, who also wanted to see the cricket match but did not have enough money.

However they had just a little more money than Anancy did. Anancy told them to meet him at the train station in the morning at 5: 00 a.m. and bring what little money they had. He told them he could get them all there if they shared the food with him, which they would buy with the extra money. They agreed. The next morning Anancy met Brother Snake and Brother Rabbit at the station.

They were excited as they saw the train coming and going. He told them he would get them to the match but they had to trust him with their money. They hesitated but then he explained that they would have spending money if they trust him. He also requested he hold all the money for safekeeping. He told them that he would keep the extra money and the tickets.

"Anancy what is the plan" they asked "I am going to get us to the match and back with one round trip ticket" he replied. They knew Anancy was a master trickster so they went with the plan but told him they would hold the extra money. Anancy walked over to the ticket booth & bought a one-way ticket to go to Kingston.

The train was ready & Anancy beckoned to them to follow him. They got on the train & Anancy led them all the way to toilet. "Anancy, is what are you doing?" asked Rabbit. Anancy told them, "Just be quiet man and watch the ride." He told them to get in quickly. Snake said to Anancy, "Mi nah ride like this go ah de match." Anancy replied "Just keep quite Snake, you will soon get your own seat. Jus watch de ride."

The train started to pull out & the conductor was coming down the aisle. "Tickets please." he shouted. He tapped on the toilet door & Anancy told Rabbit to slide the ticket under the door. The conductor took it & was on his way. Anancy & friends waited for 10 minutes so then they all left the toilet and found seats in the car. This was easy being it was the first train & it left at 5.00 a.m. On arrival at the station Rabbit and Snake bought breakfast. Anancy asked for some but they told him no they would share lunch. Anancy was angry but did not argue with them.

They got to the cricket field early and watched the set up. Rabbit & Snake bought more food.

They bought sky juice & bulla and shared none with Anancy. They ate and paid him no mind. Anancy requested food again. Snake said, "Man yuh to craven go fine yuh ownnah food." By this time Anancy realized that he was not going to get any food from them so he would have to get some for himself.

He started to devise a plan. The match had started and he continued to look food. Anancy walked over to one the vendors and told them that he wanted a patty and juice. When the man asked for money he told him his friends Snake and Rabbit would pay for it. The man walked over to Snake and Rabbit for the money. They were angry. Hold this and we will pay you the rest later. Rabbit said

"Snake since yuh have de ticket mek we leave Anancy when the match done." Snake smiled "Yes we will leave him mek im fine de money pay." The match went well and the W.I. won. Snake and Rabbit told Anancy they had to go toilet before they go.

Anancy knew they were up to something as he saw the vendor coming and they were gone for more than 15 minutes. He ran all the way to the station and the vendor was in hot pursuit. Now Snake and Rabbit were already on the train in the bathroom. Anancy got on the train sat down and waited for the train to start moving. As soon as it did he got up, went over to the restroom and changed his voice and said, "Ticket please." Snake took the ticket, slipped it under the door.

Anancy took the ticket and went back to his seat. Snake and Rabbit were doing the same thing Anancy told them, to wait 5 minutes. A little while later there was a knock on the door. "Tickets please." the person asked. Snake replied, the other conductor took our ticket." The conductor replied, "I am the only conductor on the train." As they were thrown off the train to the waiting vendors they saw Anancy sitting on the train with a big smile.

Patois Language and Anancy

Pamela Colman Smith was an author and illustrator who was born in London and spent most of her youth due to her father's job with the West India Improvement Company, the family often moved, spending time in London England, Kingston Jamaica and Brooklyn, New York.

Smith wrote and illustrated several books about Jamaican folklore, including Annancy Stories (1902) which were about Jamaican versions of tales involving the traditional African folk figure Anansi the Spider.

She illustrated children's books and collections of folk tales, ballads and verse. Her published works include Widdicombe Fair (1899), Annancy Stories (1899), The Golden Vanity and the Green Bed (1899), and Chim-Chim: Folk Stories from Jamaica (1905). She also illustrated works by other authors: Christmas Carol, by Edwin Waugh (1898), and In Chimney Corners: Merry Tales of Irish Folk-lore, by Seumas MacManus (1899).

Pamela Colman Smith heard these stories told in Jamaica by the people among themselves, or by the old nurses to their charges. And she states, "I have tried to write them down exactly as I heard them from many different people and in different parts of the island, where they vary more or less. In the hills, in the North-West, they are chiefly about birds; in other parts, about fish and rabbits, as well as the spiders Annancy and Tiger, and other animals."

Chim-Chim Folk Stories from Jamaica by Pamela Colman Smith 1905

ONCE in a long before time, before Queen Victoria came to reign over we, in dis country dere lib' Chim-Chim bird; an' him build him nes' up'pon de top of de grass, an' in de evenin', when de breeze come down from de hills, it go up an' down, up an' down, an' rock Breda Chim-Chim bird to sleep.

Now in dis country de same time, live a berry clever man, name Annancy. He was so clever dat sometime him mek' himself big, an' sometime little, an' him was half man an' half spider-a sort of jumbe man. Now dese two, Annancy an' Chim-Chim, get to know each oder in de bush; an' ebery evenin' dey play kyards together. Now dey mek' a bargain, an' dey write de bargain hout: Dat de one dat loose is to pay a fine to de one dat win-an' de one dat win is to tek a piece of flesh off de one dat loose. Now dis go on for a long time, till Annancy get quite t'in.

So now at las' Annancy him say him would only play one time more; an' dey play, an Annancy win. An' Annancy say, "Now den Breda Chim-Chimn, I gwin to tek a piece of flesh off you!" An Annancy so please-him laff!

But Chim-Chim say, "Why!" 'an fly away.
Long time Annancy try to ketch Chim-Chim, by springes, an' Calaban, an' lime' but all dis time Chim-Chim is too clever fe' him-an' he no ketch him at all!

So at las' Annancy go to him frien' Tiger (dat is anoder Spider), an' say, "I do beg you, Breda Tiger, help me ketch dat ole Chim-Chim bird; him go fly away, an' I can't ketch him at all!" - An' Tiger say- "An' what will you gib' me if I help you ketch him?"

An' Annancy say- "O me sweet frien' Tiger, I will gib' you one cow!"

Now Tiger is well fond of cow, an' him say him would do it! So him tink an' tink for a long time-an' at las' him say-"I tell you what we wi' do, Breda Annancy. I wi' lie down in de house an' play dead! an' you wi' tek a bell an' walk all roun' de town an' ring it-an' bawl out, "De great Massa Tiger is dead-de great Massa Tiger is dead." An' den all de people wi' come to de funeral-an' den you can ketch him!"

So dey write de bargain hout!

Now de nex' gran' market day, Chim-Chim come to town to get Quattie peas an' rice, an' some plantain an' salt-fish an' yam.

An' when him go trough de town-an' was in de market, him hear a bell ringin'-an' him ax' de people what it is? an' de people tell him say "De great Massa Tiger is dead."

An' Chim-Chim say- "De great Massa tiger is dead?"
An' dey say- "Yes, de great Massa Tiger is dead!"
An' Chim-Chim say-"Hi! an' when is him dead?"
An' dey say-"Yesterday forenoon."

An' Chim-Chim say- "I mus' go get me bes' coat an' go to de funeral." An' den Chim-Chim go home an' put on him second-best-two-tailed-blue-coat (fe' him best coat is too good fe' Tiger)-an' him qui-qui shoe-an' when him walk de shoe go "Buoay-soi, Buoay-soi," an' him go to Tiger house door mout. An' when him get dere him see a lot of people outside de house, a mint of people!

An' him say-"So de great Massa Tiger is dead?"
An' de say-"De great Massa Tiger is dead."
An' Chim-Chim say- "An' when is him dead?"
An' dey say- "Yesterday afternoon."
An' Chim-Chim say- "An' what is him dead wid?"
An' dey say- "De heat of de wedder!"
An' Chim-Chim say- "Hi! an' is him laugh at all since him dead?"
An' dey say- "No-a."

An' Chim-Chim say- "You no know dat man no dead at all till him do laugh?"
An' now when Tiger hear dis him gib' one big ha-ha in de house.
An' Chim-Chim say- "Hey hey, me neber hear dead man laugh yet!"
An' him fly away! An' Annancy no ketch him 'dat time, an' Tiger no get de cow.

Bumby, long time after dis, Annancy tink him wi' try one more time to ketch Chim-Chim. So him go into de bush where Chim-Chim lib, an' get in to him nes'. Now Annancy so heab'y dat when him get into de nes', de nes' go down 'pon 'de groun'! An' bumby in 'de evenin' Chim-Chim come home to him nes'-an' see it down 'pon de groun'! Him neber see it down so before! So him look at it all roun'-an' at las' him say- "Good evenin', me nes'!"

Nes' no say notting.

At las' him walk all roun' de nes' an' say-"Hi! how is dis? Ebery evein' I come home an' say, 'Good evenin', me nes',' and me nes' say, 'Good evenin', Breda Chim-Chim bird'-but dis evenin' it no

say notting!" An' den Annancy say from out de nes'- "Good evenin',
Breda Chim-Chim bird!" An' Chim-Chim say- "Hey hey! Why-me
neber' hear nes' talk yet!"

An' him fly away. An' Annancy neber ketch him to dis day!

Anancy and Plantains

A markit day but Anancy neva ave noh money, soh im siddung by di door af im cattage han im watch Tiger han Iisander di pus, Daag and Goat, han nuff adders hurry a goh markit fi buy han sell. Im neva ave nutten fi sell far im neva did du noh wurk ina di feel. Im staat fi wanda ow ima goh fine food fi im wife Crooky han im pickney dem. Han mose af all, weh ima goh fine food fi imself? No sooner im dun im thaughts, Crooky com a di door han seh tu im…yu mus goh out nung Anancy han fine sompting fi wi fi eit, wi noh ave nutten fi lunch, nutten fi dinna and tumarrow a Sunday!. A ow wi a goh manage widouten a scrap a food ina di ouse? Anancy staat fi pander a ow im a goh get sitten fi bring ina di ouse fi eit…but im seh tu har " noh worry bout nutten, mi ha goh fine sompting fi wi fi cit…mi a goh out goh wurk han get som food…han every day mi goh out wid nutten han com bak in wid sompten. Yu watch han si!

Anancy walk bout till midday, im noh fine nutten, soh im liddnung han sleep unda one shadi mango tree. Im sleep till di sun goh dung a evening han den im staat walk ome . Im walk slow far im soh shame im naa goh bak wid nutten ina im han. Im saat axe im self weh im a goh du, a weh ima goh goh fine food fi im fambily. Soh im walk han all af a sudden im com face tu face wid im ole fren Rat. Rat did ave one large hevy bunch a plantin a carry pan im ed soh till it almose a bruk im bak. Anancy eye shine wen im si di bunch a plantin, im stap han talk tu im fren Rat. Anancy seh " ow yu du mi fren Rat?…a lang time nung mi noh si yu?

Rat seh "Oh, mi staggerin alang, staggerin alang…han ow yu han di fambily?

Anancy put ann im langist face, soh lang dat im chin almose touch im toe…Im groan and shake im ed!…Haa Bredda Rat…time aad nung yu si…mi can ardly fine food fi eit fram one day tu di nex!…weh im seh dat,,tears com a im eye…but im gallang talk same way. A walk all a yestiday, and tiday and all nung mi noh fine nutten fi eit fi mi han mi fambily…Ah Br'er Rat…di children dem af fi ave so soh water fi drink tunite.

"Mi soh sarry fi ere"! Bredda Rat seh…mi nung ow mi oulda feel if mi did afi goh ome tu fi mi wife han pickney dem widouten nutten fi gi dem fi eit! Wid out even a plaintin…Ananis seh,,han im luk pan di plantin dem fi a while. Rat luk pan di plantin dem in silence tu!…Anancy seh nutten…im move tuward di plantin dem…im jus a draw close likka seh a magnet a draw im. Anancy coulden tek im eye aafa di pantin dem, but ongle fi a quick glance pan Rat face…Rat nuh seh nutten…den at last, Anancy opin im mout…" wat a lovely bunch a plantins yu ave dere Rat…weh yu get it ina dem aad time ya?"

Rat seh " Is all dat a ave lef in di field Anancy…da peas ya mus laas till di peas dem ready…han besides di plantin dem noh ready"

But dem a goh ready soon Anancy seh, dem will ready soon. Bredda Rat, gi mi two ha di plantin dem…di children dem ongle ave water fi drink fi supper tunite. All rite Anancy. Rat seh!…Jus wait a minute!!. Rat count all seven (7) a di plantin dem. Rat count dem again han at lass im bruk aff four a di smalliss plantin dem han gi dem tu Anancy. Tenk yu Bredda Rat, tenk yu mi gud fren…But Rat…a four plantin dis and is five a wi in di fambily…mi wife…di three pickney dem and miself…Rat nat even luk pan im…im ongle seh elp mi Anancy put bak di planten dem pan mi ed, han noh try fi tief aaf any more. Soh Anancy elp im and Rat goh aff pan im way but im start aff slow as di bunch di still hevy. Anancy coulda walk fass as four planten neva comin like nutten tu im. Wen im get bak tu ome…im an di four planten tu Crookey, im wife han tell har fi roast dem. Im goh outside a lie dung under di shady mango tree till Crookey caal im a tell im seh di plantin dem ready.

Anancy goh bak inside han dere was four nicely roasted plantin…im gi one to di girl and one each tu di boy dem…im gi di lass han biggess plantin tu im wife. Afta every baddy ave dem plantin im siddung very sad lukkin an im wife axe im " Anancy yu noh waan nun a di plantin?

No, Anancy seh…dere is ongle enough fi four…betta me stay hungry and yu full . But papa one a di pickney dem seh, yu nuh ungry. Anancy seh…yes chile mi hungry but yu too likkle fi fine food fi yu self…betta me stay hungry. No papa…mi affi gi yu alf a fi mi own…soh di pickney bruk aff alf a fi har plantin han gi it tu har faader…Di adder two pickney dem du di same and wen di wife si wat a gwaan she bruk aff alf a fi har own and gi Anancy tu. Soh Anancy hen up wid more dan one a di plantin dem as usual im afi out smart every baddy.

Bredda Lion and Anancy

Bredda Lion had a new bad habit that he felt was his right an privilege, being the most feared in the village. He developed the biggest belch in the whole village. Every time he ate and went to sleep at night, he would belch really loud all night and wake up the rest of the village.

Anancy loved to sleep. Next to food sleep was the next thing he loved in the whole world. Since Lion had developed this habit he has not gotten one night's sleep. Last night was the worst. Lion had belched every hour on the hour, since 8 pm that night. Anancy's eyes were blood shot red and he was angry.

He visited Bredda Rabbit and Bredda Snake to see how they were holding up. "Bredda Rabbit, how yuh doing man?" asked Anancy, as he approached Bredda Rabbit outside his home.

"Mi doing just fine." replied Bredda Rabbit.

"Yuh getting any sleep since Lion start dem big belchin?" asked Bredda Anancy.

"Yeah man, nuff sleep since mi buy dem ear muffs whey Bredda Snake tell me bout down a shop." he replied.

"Ear muffs!" Anancy exclaimed!

"Yes dem block out every sound, whey yuh nuh go buy some?" Bredda Rabbit explained.

"Is true." Anancy replied.

So he set off down to Mr. Lee's shop and bought him some ear muffs.

That night around 7: 45 pm he put on the ear muffs and went to bed.

A large "Buuuurrrrrrrrrrp" sound awoke Anancy.

"But wait," he thought to himself "dem ear muffs nah work." You see, his spider senses were just as sensitive as his ears and could pick up the sound. The others in the village did not have this type of sense so the earmuff worked for them. So again Anancy had a sleepless night.

The next morning he was very angry. He was so angry he walked over to Bredda Lion's home to talk to him.

Anancy pleaded "Bredda Lion, Mi a beg yuh please stop de all nite belching. Mi cyaan get nuh sleep a nite."

"Yuh mad Anancy? A mi run tings in dis village, an mi will stop when mi feel like." Bredda Lion replied.

"But how yuh so bad mind. Nobady cyaan sleep wid all dat noise yuh a mek." said Anancy.

"Is ongle yuh cyaan sleep. No one else is complaining." replied Bredda Lion.

Anancy was getting really upset.

"Mind yuh belch out all the food you eat for the day while you sleeping." Anancy said in anger.

"Nuh mek me dead wid laff. Mi neva hear nuttin go suh before in my life. Gwan yuh way, Anancy" Bredda Lion replied with a big smile.

At that very moment Anancy had a plan. He secretly started to follow Bredda Lion for the whole day, watching what he was eating. He took a big bag with some containers with him. Every meal that Bredda Lion had, he collected some of the same thing in a container.

That night at 8: 00pm, Bredda Anancy snuck into Bredda Lion's house under the bed. He waited to hear the first burp.

"Burrrrrrp" He snuck from under the bed and quietly placed a mixture of all the meals beside Bredda Lion's mouth.

Bredda Lion had a sensitive nose. The smell of the food mixture awoke him. He jumped out of the bed and screamed, "Lawd have mercy, all de food me eat come right back up. Whey me ago do? If this continue me will not be able to full mi stomach. I know what I will do. I will eat this mixture." So he ate the food and went back to sleep.

"Buuurrrp"Again Anancy put some more food by his mouth. And again Lion woke up and ate the food.

This continued four times. On the fourth time he put food by his mouth, Anancy snuck out of Bredda Lion's bedroom window. He crawled under the cellar to listen.

Bredda Lion ate the food but this time did not go back to sleep.

"Lawd mi bellya hat mi. Mi nuh know ef I can continue this belching business, cah mi cyaan sleep." Bredda Lion whispered under his breath. He had eaten so much food that he was in pain.

He was unable to go back to sleep.

Anancy smiled and walked back home.
This is why lions eat big meals but less frequently. Jack Mandora, mi tell yuh no lie.

Camman Sense and Breda Anancy

Wance apan a time Breda Anancy mek up im mind seh im gwine callect all a de camman sense inna de wurl. Im was tinking dat he would be de smartest smaddy in de wurl ef im do dis. So Anancy traveled all ova de wurl collecting camman sense. Im go to big countries an likkle ones. Im go to primary schools and universities. Im go to govament offices and businesses. Im go people house and dem work place. Im tek all de zillions camman sense he had collected fram around the wurl and put it a big calabash. Im tek de calabash wid im to im backyard and climbed a big gwangu tree. His plan was to store it at de tap of the tree for safety-keeping. Nobady woulda get to it but Anancy.

To mek sure it was safe Anancy tie the calabash to de front of his bady. Dis slow down im progress up de tree to a slow crawl. Im did look very clumsy a-go up de tree wid be-caw the calabash dida hamper im.

As im was slowing going up toward de top a de tree a likkle girl below called out to im. Anancy, mek you nuh tie the calabash pon you back insteada in front of yuh. It will git up de tree much fasta and ez-a.

Anancy was bex be-cah de likkle girl show im up for not thinking. She had more good sense dan him he thought. He called out to her "Mi did tink me collected all the camman sense fram all ova de wurl"

He was so angry dat im fling the calabash to the to the groung and it bust. All of the camman sense im did callect fly back to all ova de wurl.

An dat's how you and I manage to have just a likkle common sense for we-self tideh.

Jack Mandora, me tell yuh no lie!!!

Anancy and Da Fish Country

Dere was a famine in di lan han far months dem neva ave noh rain. Day after day di sum com up ina di cloudless skies, di g parch lackka caafee berry. Di tree dem also parch han brown same way, di plants in di tree dem staat fi widder away. Dere was a famine in di lan.

Well, Anancy im ungry nung and im belly feel like im neva hit fi weeks pan months, im feel like im never hit ina im llife. Im mus fine food some where, im afi go aff tu some place else fi fine som food far im really a stave nung. "If ongle mi di ave one lang coat", im sey tu imself. A oulda goh a Fish Country and preten fi bi a dockta". "Dats it"! im taut tu im self, "dats wat a gwaan du". Di ongle ting a dockta need is a black bag, a lang coat, hab a lang face".

No sooner said dan done! Missa Anancy get up nex mawning dress tu pus ina im lang coat, tall hat han black bag an set aff tu Fish country. Wen Anancy got dere, im tuk a affice, put up a signpose: M. Anancy, Surgan.

Im furst patient was a very lawge fish, shi ad many children and many gran children and many great gran children. Nung shi ave eye prablem and shi cum fi si if Anancy could elp har.

Anancy luk in har eye fram all angle, im tek lang lang, a soh im luk is soh im chat tu imself. Som a di time im even shake im haead and stap an cauf as im si adder doctors du. Anancy start tink hard, a suddinly im jus cum up han sey, " yu eye dem is weak, but a tink a can elp yu, but yu afi du exactly as a tell yu.

Hear di fule fule fish noh far shi staat ketch har fraid, "yes doctor, me will do everting yu tell mi" Soh Anancy sey, "alrite den, goh ome han goh straight tu yu bed, mek sure yu maid fix a big fire ina yu room and put on a big frying pan beside it, som coconut ile, and a sharp knife. Call mi wen yu ave everyting prepare"

Di fat fish urry ome and du exactly wat Anancy tell har fi du, soh wen everyting ready shi sen goh caal Anancy. Soh Anancy ketch a yard and sey tu di fambily, " all a unnu mus leave di room. A afi lack di door. Unnu mus nat try fi open it, nar luk inside it, but unnu mus listen carefully han wen unnu ear di frying pan a fry unnu mus sey, fee fee han stamp unnu fut han sing da sang ya. Bim, Bam,mi grannie eye well, ooh,
Bim, Bam,mi grannie eyc wcll, ooh,
Bim, Bam,mi grannie eye well, ooh,

Unnu mus mek up ole eep a noise, unni ear mi? Soh since di sang neva ard fi lern, di ole a di fish dem ketch aan quick! But Anancy smarter dan dem, im noh leave nutten tu chance, so as soon as im feel sey dem lern di sang gud enough, im leave a goh inside an lack di door.
Im put di frying pan pan di fire and put di ile ina it. Wen di ile staat bwile, han sizzle, im caal out "fee fee". As di frying pan bwile, Anancy tek di fat fish and put it ina di pan wile di fule fule fish dem dey outside a sing " Bim Bam…pan di tap a dem vice.

Soh dem sing, soh Anancy nam di fish, wen im belly full nung, im wipe im mout pan di sheet and lick im lip soh wen im leaving nobaddy ould know sey im was eating somptomg. Nung im afi fine a wey fi get out before di fambily ketch up pan im. Im staat tink ard nung, a wey im ago du? Im cover di bone dem wid di sheet pick up im bag put aan a lang face and mek im exit.

Wen im goh outside im sey tu di likkle fule fule fish dem, all is well di apperation was a success, but unnu mus nat goh inside dere far at least two hours. Unnu ave bin making ole eep a nise soh unnu mus nung bi still and nung yu all afi pay mi mi fee.

Soh di fule fule fish dem pay im and im set aaff on im journey, im nung im mus leave Fish Country quick soh im affi fine di shartest way out. Dat ould mean im afi c**** di river wid a ole eep a alligators. Ow im a go get c**** dat nung? Same time Anancy saw bredder Dog pan di odder side af di river.

"Ahh! breddaog" Anancy sey, yu glad fi si me? "No!" bark bredda dog. Oh!!, but a sure yu ould bi glad if yu know omuch money mi ave, shaking di bag in front a bredda dog. "Mek mi si it", barked bredda dog, no bredda dog, mi afi c**** dis ya river ya. "C**** nung" bredda dog bark.
But di alligators dem will eit mi? said Anancy. Leave dat tu me, di dog staat run alang di river banking, barking as im go. Di greedy alligators fallow bak a di dog tinking dat im oulda jump in di water. Wile di dog a du fi im ting, Anancy dash c**** di river and was soon safe on di odder side.

Since bredda dog was stronger dan im, im lef di bag a money by the ford. Bredda dog was very pleased wid imself. Wen di fish dem arrive at di banking af di river, which was a far as could goh, dey saw Anancy. But dem could'nt du a ting, Anancy was already running thru di farest singing "Bim Bam…."

Anancy and the Doctor

Anancy heard that the princess had a injury and had to go to the hospital. There was no spaces left in the hospital except the bed next to the princess.

One day Anancy went to a doctor and said, "May I come in?" "NO, there's nothing wrong with you," said the doctor.

Then Anancy fell over on purpose and broke his leg. The doctor had to take him in now. The doctor put him in the bed next to the princess and they fell in love.

So the princess went up to the doctor and said, "I don't want to marry you anymore because I 've met Anancy and I love him, also your're not my type."

Then the doctor went mad with rage and smoke came out of his ears. He ran out of the room. Anancy and the princess got married in the hospital. When they went out of the hospital there was a golden carriage waiting for them and over 60 monkeys pulling it along. The doctor was very jealous and so frustrated that he killed someone and got put in jail for life.

Anancy and the princess lived happily ever after.
The End

The Fish Basket
by George Parkes, Mandeville

One great hungry time. Anansi couldn't get anyt'ing to eat, so he take up his hand-basket an' a big pot an' went down to the sea-side to catch fish. When he reach there, he make up a large fire and put the pot on the fire, an' say, "Come, big fish!"

He catch some big fish put them aside. He said, "Big fish go, make little fish come!" He then catch the little fish. He say, "Little fish go, make big fish come!" an' say, "Big fish go, make little fish come!"

He then catch the pot full an' his hand-basket. He bile the pot full and sit down and eat it off; he then started home back with the pot on his head and the basket. Reaching a little way, he hide the pot away in the bush an take the basket along with him now.

While going along, he meet up Tiger. Now Tiger is a very rough man an' Anansi 'fraid of him. Tiger said to him, "What you have in that basket, sah?"—speak to him very rough. Anansi speak in a very feeble voice, say, "Nothing, sah! Nothing, sah!"

So both of them pass each other, an' when they went on a little way, Tiger hide in the bush watching Anansi. Anansi then sit down underneath a tree, open his basket, take out the fishes one one, and say, "Pretty little yallah-tail this!" an' put it aside; he take out a snapper an' say, "Pretty little snapper this!" an' put it one side; he take out a jack-fish an' say, "Pretty little jack-fish!" an' put it one side.

Tiger then run up an' say, "Think you havn't not'ing in that basket, sah!" Anansi say, "I jus' going down to the sea have a bathe, sah, an' I catch them few 'itte fishes." Tiger say, "Give it to me here, sah!"—talk in a very rough manner. An' Tiger take it an' eat them all an' spit up the bones.

Anansi then take up the bones an' eat them, an' while eating he grumble an' say, "But look me bwoy labor do!" Tiger say, "What you say?" Anansi say, "Fly humbug me face, sah!" (Brushing his face).

So booth of them start to go home now with the empty basket, but this time Anansi was studying for Tiger. When he reach part of the way, Anansi see a fruit-tree. Anansi say, "What a pretty fruit-tree!" (looking up in the tree).

Tiger say, "Climb it, sah!" (in a rough manner). So when Anansi go up an' pull some of the fruit, at that time Tiger was standing underneath the tree. Anansi look down on Tiger head an' said,

"Look lice in a Brar Tiger head!" Tiger said, "Come down an' ketch it, sah!"
Anansi come down an' said to Tiger he kyan't ketch it without he lean on the tree. Tiger said,

"Lean on the tree, sah!" The hair on Tiger head is very long. So while Anansi ketchin' the lice, Tiger fell asleep. Anansi now take the hair an' lash it round the tree tie up Tiger on the tree. After he done that he wake up Tiger an' say that he kyan't ketch any more.

Tiger in a rough manner say, "Come an' ketch it, sah!" Anansi say, "I won't!" So Anansi run off, Tiger spring after him, an' fin' out that his hair is tied on the tree. So Tiger say, "Come an' loose me, sah!" Anansi say. "I won't!" an' Anansi sing now,

"See how Anansi tie Tiger,

See how Anansi tie Tiger,

Tie him like a hog, Tiger,

See how Anansi tie Tiger,

Tie him like a hog, Tiger!"

An' Anansi leave him go home, am' a hunter-man come an' see Tiger tie on the tree, make kill him.

The Storm
by Vivian-Bailey, Mandeville

Brer Tiger got a mango-tree in his place. Brer Nansi go an' ask if he could sell him a ha' penny wort' of mango. Brer Tiger say no. Brer Nansi well want de mango. Brer Nansi say, "Law pass dat eb'ry man have tree mus' tie on it 'cause going to get a heavy storm." Brer Tiger say, well, mus' tie him to de mango-tree. After Brer Nansi tie Tiger, climb up in de mango-tree, an' eb'ry mango he eat tak it an' lick Brer Tiger on de head. After he eat done, he shake off all de ripe mango an' pick dem up go away leave Brer Tiger tie up on de mango-tree.

Brer Tiger see Brer But pass an' ask Brer But to loose him. Brer But say dat he kyan't stop. Brer Tiger see Brer Ant passing ask Brer Ant to loose him; Brer Ant say he kyan't depon[1] haste. Brer Tiger see Brer Duck-ants passing an' ask him fe loose him. An' don' know if him will loose him, for don' know if him will put up wid him slowness, for Duck-ants is a very slow man. After him loose him, Brer Tiger tell him many t'anks an' tell him mus' never let him hear any of Duck-ants's frien's pass him an' don' call up "How-dy-do."

Brer Nansi in a cotton tree were listening when dey talking. De nex' evening, Brer Nansi go to Brer Tiger yard an' knock at de door. An' say, "Who is deah?" an' say, "Mr. Duck-ants's brudder." An' dey tak him in an' mak much of him, get up tea because it was Mr. Duck-ants's brudder, an' after dat go to bed. In de morning provide tea for Mr. Duck-ants 'fore he wake, an' when he wake an' was washin' his face he got to tak off his hat. An' Brer Nansi is a man wid a bald head, an' dey got to fin' out it was Brer Nansi an' dey run him out of de house.

The Kings Two Daughters
by William Forbes, Dry River

Deh was Anansi. He go out an' court two young lady was de king daughter an' mak dem a fool, an' dem ketch him an' tie him, an' de two sister go an' look a bundle a wood fe go an' mak a fire under a copper fe bu'n him wid hot water. An' after when dem gone, he see Tiger was coming. Anansi said, "Lawd! Brar Tiger, I get into trouble heah!" An' said, "Fe wha'?" An' say, "King daughter wan' lib wid dem, come tie me." Tiger say, 'You fool, mak y' loose an' tie me!"

Anansi tie Tiger dere now an' Anansi go to a grass-root an' dodge. An' when de misses go t'row down de wood at de fireside, de littlest one say, "Sister! sister! look de little uncle wha' we tie heah, him tu'n a big uncle now!" Sister say, "I soon 'big uncle' him!" an' dem mak up de fire bu'n up de water, tak two ladle an' dem dashey upon Tiger. An' him jump, an' jump, pop de rope, tumble dump on de grass-root whe' Anansi was. Anansi laugh "Tissin, tissin, tissin!"

An' Tiger jump 'pon Anansi, say, "We mus' go look wood gwine to bu'n your back!" Tiger see some good wood on a cotton-tree well dry, an' Tiger say, "I don' care wha' you do!"
An' when Anansi go tip on cotton-tree, him chop one of de limb pum! an' 'top, an' chop again pum! an' holla, "None!" Tiger say, "Cut de wood, man!" An' holla again, "None!" Tiger said, "Cut de wood, I tell you, come down mak I bu'n you." Anansi say, "You stan' upon de bottom say 'cut de wood, but you know Hunter-man

look fe you las' yeah track? Wha' you t'ink upon dis yeah track worse!" an' Tiger run, Anansi say, "He run, Massa Hunter-man, gone up on hill-side, gone dodge!" He move from dere gone on ribber-side. Anansi holla, "Him gone, Massa Hunterman, a ribber!" Tiger wheel back. An' Anansi holla to him say go to a sink-hole, an' Anansi get rid of him an' come off. Jack man dora!

The Gub-Gub Peas
by George Parkes, Mandeville

A man plant a big field of gub-gub peas.[Navy Beans] He got a watchman put there. This watchman can't read. The peas grow lovely an' bear lovely; everybody pass by, in love with the peas. Anansi himself pass an' want to have some. He beg the watchman, but the watchman refuse to give him. He went an' pick up an' old envelope, present it to the watchman an' say the master say to give the watchman.

The watchman say, "The master know that I cannot read an' he sen' this thing come an' give me?" Anansi say, "I will read it for you." He said, "Hear what it say! The master say, 'You mus' tie Mr. Anansi at the fattest part of the gub-gub peas an' when the belly full, let him go.'" The watchman did so; when Anansi belly full, Anansi call to the watchman, an' the watchman let him go.

After Anansi gone, the master of the peas come an' ask the watchman what was the matter with the peas. The watchman tol' him. Master say he see no man, no man came to him an' he send no letter, an' if a man come to him like that, he mus' tie him in the peas but no let him away till he come.

The nex' day, Anansi come back with the same letter an' say, "Master say, give you this." Anansi read the same letter, an' watchman tie Anansi in the peas. An' when Anansi belly full, him call to the watchman to let him go, but watchman refuse. Anansi call out a second time, "Come, let me go!" The watchman say, "No, you don' go!" Anansi say, 'If you don' let me go, I spit on the groun' an' you rotten!" Watchman get frighten an' untie him.

Few minutes after that the master came; an' tol' him if he come back the nex' time, no matter what he say, hol' him. The nex' day, Anansi came back with the same letter an' read the same story to the man.

The man tie him in the peas, an', after him belly full, he call to the man to let him go; but the man refuse,—all that he say he refuse until the master arrive.

The master take Anansi an' carry him to his yard an' tie him up to a tree, take a big iron an' put it in the fire to hot. Now while the iron was heating, Anansi was crying. Lion was passing then, see Anansi tie up underneath the tree, ask him what cause him to be tied there.

Anansi said to Lion from since him born he never hol' knife an' fork, an' de people wan' him now to hol' knife an' fork. Lion said to Anansi, "You too wort'less man! me can hol' it.
I will loose you and then you tie me there." So Lion loose Anansi an' Anansi tied Lion to the tree. So Anansi went away, now, far into the bush an' climb upon a tree to see what taking place.

When the master came out, instead of seeing Anansi he see Lion.
He took out the hot iron out of the fire an' shove it in in Lion ear.
An Lion make a plunge an' pop the rope an' away gallop in the bush an' stan' up underneath the same tree where Anansi was.

Anansi got frighten an' begin to tremble an' shake the tree, Lion then hol' up his head an' see Anansi.

He called for Anansi to come down. Anansi shout to the people, "See de man who you lookin' fe! see de man underneat' de tree!" An' Lion gallop away an' live in the bush until now, an' Anansi get free.

Tiger as Riding Horse
by William Forbes, Dry River

Tiger was walking to a yard an' see two young misses, an' he was courting one of de young misses. An' as Anansi hear, Anansi go up to yard where de young misses is; an' dey ax him said, "Mr. Anansi, you see Mr. Tiger?" An' said, "O yes! I see Mr. Tiger, but I tell you, missus, Tiger is me fader ol' ridin'-horse." An' when Tiger come to misses, dem tell him. An' said him gwine Anansi, mak him come an' prove witness befo' him face how he is fader ol' ridin'-horse!

An' when him come call Anansi, say, "Want you to come prove dis t'ing you say 'fore de misses," Anansi say, "I nebber say so! but I kyan' walk at all.," Tiger said, "If I hab to carry you 'pon me back, I will carry you go!" Anansi said, "Well, I wi' go." Anansi go tak out him saddle, Tiger say, "What you gwine do wid saddle?" Anansi say, "To put me foot down in de stirrup so when I gwine fall down, I weak, I can catch up." An' tak him bridle. Tiger say, "What you gwine do wid it?" Say, "Gwine put it in you mout', when I gwine to fa' down I can catch up." Tiger say, "I don' care what you do, mus' put it on!"

An' him go back an' tak horse-whip. An' say, "Wha' you gwine do wid de horsewhip?" An' say, "Fe when de fly come, fan de fly." An' put on two pair of 'pur. An' say, "Wha' you gwine do wid 'pur?" An' say, "if I don' put on de 'pur, me foot wi' cramp." An' come close to yard an' close in wid de 'pur an' horse-whip, an' mak him gallop into de yard. An' say, "Carry him in to stable, sah! I mak you to know what Anansi say true to de fac', is me fader ol' ridin'-horse."

Tiger tak to wood, Anansi sing a'ter him, "Po' Tiger dead an' gone!"

Si-lay-na, Si-lay-na, Si-lay-na bom, Eb-ry-bod-y
Si-lay-na, Si-lay-na, Si-lay-na bom, Si-lay-na, Si-lay-na.
Po' Ti-ger dead and gone, Si-lay-na, Si-lay-na, Si-lay-na,
Eb-ry-bod-y go look fo' dem wife, Si-lay-na, Si-lay-na,
Eb-ry-bod-y go look fo' dem wife, Si-lay-na, Si-lay-na, Si-lay-na bom.

Tiger Sheep-Skin Suit
by George Parkes, Mandeville

Anansi was a head-man for a man by the name of Mr. Mighty, who employed Anansi for the purpose of minding some sheep. The sheep numbered about two thousand. And from the first day Anansi took over the sheep, the man began to miss one. An' he steal them until he leave only one. Well, Mr. Mighty would like to find out how the sheep go. He say to Anansi he would give his best daughter and two hundred pound to find out how the sheep go.

Anansi say the best way to find it out is to make a ball. Anansi have a friend name of Tiger, call him 'Brar Tiger'. He went to Tiger an' tell him Mr. Mighty promise to give his daughter an' two hundred pound to whomsoever tell how the sheep go. Anansi now is a fiddler, an' he say that he will play the fiddle an' Tiger play the tambourine, but before he go to the ball he will give Tiger a sheepskin coat, sheepskin trousers, a sheepskin cap, a sheepskin boot; an' when him, Tiger, hear him play,

'Mister Mighty loss him sheep,
It stan' lik' a Tiger t'iefee," him, Tiger, mustn't think him the same one; it's one clear out the country. And he is to play his tambourine, say,

"Fe tre-ew, bredder, fe tre-ew,
it 'tan lik' a it mak me clo'es."

Now then, Anansi go back to Mr. Mighty an' tol' him that there is a man coming to the ball wearing a suit of sheep-skin clo'es,—dat is the man who steal the sheep.

Mr. Mighty give out invitation to all the high folks, all the ladies and gentlemen all aroun', to attend the ball at that same date. The night of the ball, Anansi went with his fiddle an' Tiger with his tambourine in the suit of sheep-skin clo'es. At the time fix, Anansi tune up his fiddle, 'he-rum, te-rum, she-rum.' Tiger now trim the tambourine, 'ring-ping, ring-ping, ring-pong, pe-ring-ping, double-ping, tong!' Anansi says, "Gentlemen an' ladies, ketch yo' pardner!" Anansi play,

> "Mr. Mighty loss him sheep,
> Mr. Mighty loss him sheep,
> Mr. Mighty loss him sheep,
> Tiger say, It stan' lik' a Tiger t'iefee."

> Tiger say,
> "Fe tre-ew, bredder, fe tre-ew,
> Fe tre-ew, bredder, fe tre-ew,
> Fe tre-ew, bredder, fe tre-ew,
> It 'tan' lik' a it mak me clo'es."

Anansi go to Mr. Mighty an' say, "Me an' dat man workin' an' I didn't know he was such a t'ief! he steal de sheep till he tak skin an' all mak him clo'es!" An' as they were going back to their places Anansi say, "Hell after you t'-night, only t'ing you don't know!" Tiger say, "What you say, Bra'?"—"Me say, you not playing strong enough, you mus' play up stronger!"

Anansi say again, "Gentlemen an' ladies, ketch 'em a pardner!" an' sing,

"Mr. Mighty loss him sheep,
It 'tan' lik' a Tiger t'iefee."

Tiger say,
"Fe tre-ew, bredder, fe tre-ew,

It 'tan' lik' a it mak me clo'es".
Mr. Mighty got right up an' said to Tiger, "Yes, that is the man what steal all my sheep!" Tiger say, "No!!" Anansi say, "Yes, that is the man what steal all the sheep, an' I an' that man eatin' an' I didn't know that man was such a t'ief!" An' Tiger was arrested an' got ten years in prison, an' Anansi get the two hundred pounds an' the best daughter to marry to,

The Escape
by Joseph Macfarlane, Moneague, St. Ann

One day was an old lady name Mis' Madder, had twenty sheep. Mr. Anansi went an' gi' her a hen an', couple week after, Mr. Anansi went back fe de hen. An' said, "Didn't you gi' me de hen, Mr. Anansi?" An' said, "Oh, no! Missus, me hen wud have hegg, hegg, on hegg, chicken on chicken!" An' said, "De only t'ing I can do' Mr. Anansi, go in de sheep-pen an' tak a sheep!" It went on till de nineteen was gone, leave one. Tiger says, "Mis' Madder, I'll kill de sheep tak a half an' ketch Mr. Anansi." Tiger kill i', put 'e skin over himself. When Mr. Anansi come, Tiger bawl like a sheep "Ba-a-a-a!" Miss Madder say, "All right, Mr. Anansi, I don' wan' to hear any more talkin'; tak' de las' sheep an' go." Anansi say, "T'ank you, Miss Madder, won' come back an' worry you fe no more fowl!"

When he went off, under way said, "Yah! dis sheep hebby, sah!" Went home, de wife an' chil'ren sit roun' him wid bowl an' knife. Mr. Anansi tak de knife cut de t'roat an' say, "Lawd! me wife, dis fellow fat till no hav any blood!" Cut de belly come down, Tiger jump out hold him. Mr. Anansi say, "He! he! Brar Tiger, wha' you do?" Tiger say, "Miss Madder ha' twenty sheep an' if me no tie you, him wi' say you an' me eat dem." Anansi say, "If dem tak dem big banana trash tie me, I wi' be glad, but if dey could a tak dat 'itte bit o' banana t'read tie me, I should be so sorry!" An' dey tie him wid de small banana trash an' t'row into de sea, an' he jus' open his leg an' run under water. An' from dat time you see Anansi running under water.

The Substitute
by Samuel Christie, St. Ann's Bay

Anansi is a smart one, very smart, likes to do unfair business. So one day was walking t'ru a lady property an' kill a little bird; so him pass de lady yard an' say, "Missus, me beg you mak little bird stan' till me come back?" Lady said, "Put it down, Anansi." Lef' de bird an' he never come back till he know de bird spile. De lady t'row de bird. He come back, say, "Missus, me jus' call fe de litt'e bird me lef' t'odder day. Say, "Anansi, de bird spoil an' me t'row it away!"— "No, missus, you kyan' t'row 'way me bird! Jus' call an' me want i'!" Lady say, "Well, Anansi, before you ill-treat me, go in de sheep-pen an' tak a sheep."

Anansi was quite glad fe dat, get a sheep fe de bird! An' go down fin' a sheep-pen wid plenty of sheep. Anansi go an' tak dat one, an' after dat, ev'ry night he tak one. Lady fin' all de sheep was los', so tell de head man mus' keep watch of de sheep-pen. So de head-man was Tiger. Tiger tak out dat sheep was in de sheep-pen an' dress himself wid sheep-skin. Anansi have suspicion an' get a frien' to go wid him dat night, ask de frien' to catch de sheep. So as him frien' t'row on de rope on Tiger head, Anansi fin' it was Tiger an' him ask excuse, go to a good distance where can mak escape, holla, "Dat somet'ing you ketch deh no sheep,—Brar Tiger!"

Tiger tie de frien' carry him up to de yard tell de mistress dis is de man been destroying de sheep all de time!

In the House-Top
by Thomas White,
Maroon Town, Cock-pit Country

Mr. Goolin pay Anansi a hundred poun' to mak him wife talk, an' Anansi was live upon Mr. Goolin ev'ry day an' go to Mr. Goolin yard ev'ry day fe money. Mr. Goolin get tired of Anansi an' couldn't get rid of Anansi out of him yard.

Tiger hear, an' go to Mr. Goolin tell him dat him will stop Anansi from comin' in yard. An' so Tiger did; Tiger turn a big barrow an' go lie down in de common. Anansi come now an' say, "Mawnin', Mr. Goolin." Mr. Goolin say, "Mawnin', Mr. Anansi. "Anansi says, "I might well tell you de trut'! De amount of what money you pay me fe yo' wife, it is not enough!'

Mr. Goolin says, "Well, I have no more money to pay you again." Anansi says, "O Mr. Goolin! you couldn't tell me a word as dat!" Mr. Goolin says to Anansi, "Mr. Anansi, all I can do fe you, go in de common see a big barrow lie down dere. You can go catch it."
Anansi tek him rope an' go in de common an' him tie de big barrow an' him put it jus' right across him shoulder. An' he was goin' along till him ketch part of de way, him says to himself, "Ha! if I didn't cunnie, I wouldn't get dis big barrow t'-day." So look an' see a long beard come down on him face. Dat was Tiger! Tiger go fe shake him an' he say, "O Brar Tiger, no shake! no shake! no shake!"

Anansi run fe him house an', when he get near, him holler to him wife say, "Shet de back do', open de front do', Brar Tiger come!" Wife say, "Wha' you say? say wash out de pot?"—"No! shet de back do, open de front do'!"—"Wha' you say? put on de pot, come?" Him say, "No-o-o! s-h-e-t de b-a-c-k d-o-o-o! o-p-e-n de f-r-o-n-t d-o-o-o-o!"

Wife put up all dem chil'ren quite a-top, and, as Anansi put down Tiger, Anansi fly up a-top, too.

An' Tiger was layin' down in de hall middle, an' all de chil'ren an' de wife, dem all upon house-top. Anansi have six chil'ren. De chil' one of dem, says he hungry. As de chil' say he hungry, Anansi shove down dat chil' t' Brar Tiger.

Tiger swallow him. Anodder cry out hungry again; Anansi shove him down, Tiger swallow him. Anodder one cry hungry again; Anansi shove him down gi' Tiger, Tiger swallow him. Dch's t'ree gone. Him was deh again till anodder one cry hungry; Anansi shove him down to Tiger, Tiger swallow him.

For a good time again de odder one cry out hungry; Anansi shove him down gi' Tiger, Tiger swallow him. Good time again, de las' chil' lef', him cry hungry. Anansi shove him down gi' Tiger, Tiger swallow him. Lef' him an' him wife, two single, now. Anansi fell in sleep. De wife tak needle an' t'read an' sew Anansi trouser-foot upon her frock-tail.

When Anansi wake out of sleep, him wife cry hungry now. Anansi shove down him wife to give Tiger. De woman frock-tail sew up on Anansi trouser-foot an' ketch him up back. An' de lady was deh for a good time until him cry hungry again an' Anansi shove him down gi' Tiger an' Tiger swallow Mrs. Anansi.

Anansi was deh on de house-top until he feel hungry now. An' says to Tiger, "Brar Tiger, you know what you do? I's a man dat's so fat, if I drop on de bare eart' I's goin' to mash up; so if you want me to eat, you want to cut a whole heap a dry trash." An' Tiger went an' cut a whole heap a dry trash an' carried de dry trash come an' he t'rown de dry trash.

Anansi said to Tiger, "Brar Tiger, ketch, ketch, ketch, comin' down!" An' Anansi let himself off of de house-top an' drop in de trash, an' Tiger was upon hard sarchin' an' couldn't fin' Anansi until t'-day!

Jack man dora, choose none!

Tiger's Breakfast
by Richard Morgan, Santa Cruz Mountains

One day, Hanansi go Tiger house an' eat breakfas' every day, an' tell Tiger, say, "Brar Tiger, to-morrow you mus' come a my house; but when you hear me makin' noise you mus' come, for dat time breakfas' is on, but when you hear me stay still you mustn't come at all."

So when Tiger go, Hanansi eat done. And say, "Brar Tiger, you foot short!" Tiger say, "No, me no hear you mak noise!" Hanansi say, "No, so me said, for when man makin' noise he kyan' eat." An' say, "Well, nex' day come back."

When Tiger come, Hanansi tak shame, gi' him little breakfas' but say, "Brar Tiger, when we go fe eat, when I say 'Nyammy nyammy nyammy' you mus' say, 'Nyam a wha' eat'."So Hanansi stay deh eat everyt'ing, Tiger never get one.

Tiger study fe him. Nex' day he go to Tiger yard. When Tiger gi' him breakfast an' gi' him enough meat he said to Tiger, "Brar Tiger, a whe' you get meat every day so?"
Tiger said, "You know how me come by dis meat? When I see a cow lie down, I go up an' run me ban' inside of de cow an' hol' de man tripe, so I never out of meat."

So Hanansi went his way an' do de same. De cow frighten on de hill-side an' turn head right down to lowland. Hanansi say, "Do, Brar Cow, don't shut up me han'!"

Cow fasten de han' de better an' gallop right down de hill an' drag Hanansi over de stone. Dat's de reason let you see Hanansi belly white.

Eggs and Scorpions
by William Forbes,
Dry River, Cock-pit Country

Blinkie an' Anansi was gwine in a wood. Dem gwine in a wood fe go look egg, bird egg. An' Anansi tell Blinkie when little bird say, "Who wan' little egg?" Blinkie fe say him want little egg, an' when de big bird say, "Who wan' big egg?" Anansi say, "Me wan' big egg!" An' in de night when he get all de big egg, Blinkie get vex' an' lef' Anansi in de bush an' him fly away wid de light.

An' Anansi come a Tiger house in a night. Tiger had a sheep in yard. Anansi say, "Brar Tiger, if you gi' me dinner fe eat t'-night, I gi' you all de egg." An' Tiger say yes, an' Tiger go to de sheep an' say, "Lay out, lay out, sheep!" He lay out roas' fowl, roas' duck, an' all sort a t'ings. Anansi get at it.

When he eat, say want to sleep Tiger house. Tiger set 'corpion roun' de egg. When Anansi put han' in to tak de egg, 'corpion bite him. An' holla, "Aye-e-e!" Tiger say, "Brar Anansi, wha' ha' you?" An' say, 'Me t'ree litt'e pickney an' me wife mak me a cry. Den, when Tiger gone t' bed, he t'ief away de sheep.

Tiger' Bone Hole
by William Forbes,
Dry River, Cock-pit Country

Tiger had a big pot o' meat, an' him boil an' let' it gone a groun'. An' he have a bone-hole; when he ate de meat, t'row it into de hole. An' Anansi tak him wife an' t'ree pickney an' he say dey five gwine to de house an' get into de pot eat de meat.

An' after dey hear Tiger was coming, him an' him wife an' de t'ree pickney, five of dem, go in de hole. An' Tiger come an' say, "Not a creetur nyam dis meat but Brar Nansi!" An' Tiger begin now eat meat, an' de first bone him t'row into de hole, him knock one of de pickney.
An' as he go fe holla, Anansi says, "Shut yo' mout', sir, don' cry!" An' he eat again, t'row out anodder bone, knock anodder pickney. As him go fe cry, say "Shut yo' mout', sir!" As he eat anodder bone again, he knock de las' pickney, mak t'ree.

Tell him say him mustn't cry. Ate anodder bone an' t'row it in de hole, knock de mudder. As him go fe cry, say, "Shut yo' mout'!" An' de las' bone he eat, knock Anansi in a head.
Anansi say, "Mak we all holla now in a de hole!" So dey all holla "Yee! yee-e-e!" in a de hole, an' as dey holla, Tiger get frighten' an' run let' de house, an Anansi an' wife an pickney come out tak all de meat go away, run him out of his house 'count of dat bone-hole!

Jack man dora!

The Christening
by Charles Wright,
Maroon Town, Cock-pit Country

Anansi an' Tiger bot' of them fin' one keg of butter. Anansi says to Tiger, "Let us hide it in the bushes." Some days after, Anansi says to Tiger, "I receive a letter for a christening."

When he return, Tiger ask him the name of the chile. He says the name is "Top take off."

Another week came again. He say receive another letter for another christening.

After he come back, Tiger ask him what's the name of the chile again. He says, "Catch in de middle," An' the las' week he went back for another christening.

Tiger ask him when he come back what's the name of the chile. He says, "Lick clean."

Now he says, "Tiger, let us go look for this keg of butter." He carried Tiger all over the place walkin' until he get tired, an' when he nearly catch to the place where they hid the butter he said,

"Tiger, we are tired, let us go for a sleep,!"

An' after Tiger was sleeping, he went to the keg, he took a bit of stick an' he scrape as much as he can get from the keg, an' he wipe a little on Tiger mouth an' he wipe a little at the tail.

Then he climb a tall tree now and he make a wonderful alarm that Tiger eat butter until he melt butter!

Throwing Away Knives
Then You Can't Eat Pineapple
by Benjamin Collins, Mandeville

Once upon a time Brer Tiger an' Brer Anansi was gwine on. Brer Anansi tell Brer Tiger says, "Brer Tiger, I'm gwine to t'row away my knife an' when you see I t'row away mine, you mus' t'row away yours, too."

Brer Anansi tak somet'ing an' t'row it away, an' Brer Tiger tak his knife an' t'row it away.

An' when dem reach de fiel' to eat pine, deh comes Brer Nansi had his knife, he was eating pine, an 'Brer Tiger didn't get none.

Brer Nansi say to Brer Tiger, "Brer Tiger, no man a knife nyam pine; no man no have knife no nyam pine!"

Sheep and Anansi
by William Forbes,
Dry River, Cock-pit Country

Mr. Anansi an' Mr. Sheep going out walking over de country. Carry two spoon; Sheep carry one, Anansi carry one. Anansi tell Sheep, "Mr. Sheep, lef' you spoon here, don' carry it."

Den go to de second house an' get some breakfas' again. After him get de breakfas' him say, "Mr. Sheep, where you spoon?" An' said, "Don't you tell me to lef' it at de firs' house?"—"You mus' go back for it now!"

Mr. Sheep gone for it, him eat off all de breakfas'. An' said, "Come, Mr. Sheep, but you mus' let' you spoon."—"Me won't carry it at all." Den go up to de nex't yard an' get dinner now. Night is coming. An' said, "Mr. Sheep, where is you' 'poon?" An' said, "I lef' it at de las' yard you eat."

Well, den, Sheep have to go back fe his spoon again; tell Sheep come back again an' Anansi eat off de dinner. Sheep couldn't get not'ing to eat.

Monkey and Anansi
by Samuel Christie, St. Anne's Bay

Anansi and Monkey were travelling; they were two good friends together. Anansi ask Monkey, "Brer Monkey, how much cunnie you have?" Said, "Brer, me have plenty plenty!"

Anansi said, "Brer, me only have one one-half; I keep the one fe meself an' give me friend the half."

Trabble on, trabble on, until they see Tiger in one deep hole. Anansi say, "Brer Monkey, you have plenty cunnie an' long tail; sen' down tail into the hole an' help Brer Tiger!"

While him sen' down him tail, Anansi climb one tree. Tiger come out of the hole now, lay hold on Monkey, say, "I nyam you t'-day!" Anansi on the tree laughing.

Monkey into a fix now, don't know how to get away. So Anansi call out to Tiger, "Brer Tiger, you ketch Monkey now you gwine eat him?"

Tiger say, "Yes, I gwine eat him." Anansi say, "Do like me, now. Open you two hand an' clap wid joy, say, 'I get Monkey!'"

That time he open his two hand, Monkey get free. Tiger run after Monkey, Anansi mak his way down from the tree, go home.

Goat, Anansi and Tiger
by Henry Spence, Bog, Westmoreland

Anansi and Tiger go out hunting one day. Tiger catch one wild goat, Anansi no catch one.

Anansi say to him, "Brar Tiger, wha' you say when you catch dis goat?" So Tiger say, "Not'ing!"

Anansi say, "Brar Tiger, nex' time when you catch goat so, you mus' put goat under yo' arm an' knockey han' at top say, 'T'ank de Lord!'"

An' Tiger did so an' de goat get away gone; de two lose.

Rabbit and Anansi
by Susan Watkins, Claremont, St. Ann

Brar Nansi and Brar Rabbit went for a walk one day. Brar Rabbit ask Brar Anansi to show him 'daytime trouble'. An' while dey go on, Brar Anansi saw Tiger den wid a lot of young Tiger in it.

Brar Anansi took out one an' kill it an' give Rabbit a basket wid a piece of de Tiger's meat to carry for de Tiger's fader, an' took Rabbit along wid him to Tiger's house an' tol' Brar Rabbit to han' Tiger de basket. Anansi run, an' Tiger catch at Rabbit to kill him, but he get away.

Brar Anansi run up a tree an' say, "Run, Brar Rabbit, run! run fe stone-hole!" Took a razor an' give it to Rabbit. An' Tiger got up a lot of men to get Rabbit out de hole an' Tiger sent for Reindeer to dig him out, as he had a long neck to put down his head an' dig him out; but Anansi tol' Rabbit when Reindeer put down his head in de hole, he mus' tak de razor an' cut it off.

A lot of people gadder to see Reindeer tak Rabbit out of de hole, but instead, Reindeer head was taken off an' he drop an' was dead an' de whole crowd run away wid fright.

After Rabbit come out, Brar Nansi say to him, "Brar Rabbit, so 'daytime trouble' stay. So, as long as you live, never ask anybody to show it to you again!"

Rat and Anansi
by Moses Hendricks, Mandeville

Rat and Anansi went out one day. They came across Tiger's four children,—Anansi knew exactly where they was. He had a handbasket, Rat had one. So Anansi said, "Brer, two fe me, two fe you!" Anansi tak up one, mak the attempt as if he going to kill it but he didn't do so, put it in his basket alive.

Rat t'ot Anansi kill it, an' he tak up his now an' kill it an' put it in his basket. Anansi did the same with the second one,—didn't kill it, put it in his basket. Pat took up the other one an' him kill it. So Rat had two dead ones an' Anansi had his alive.

Anansi knew exactly which way Tiger would walk coming home. They met Tiger. Said, "Brer Tiger, I see yo' baby them Crying hungry, I tak them up come meet you. I carry two, Brer Rat two." Tiger lay down now to nurse them. Anansi took out one alive.

Rat took out one dead, got frightened. Tiger looks cross. Anansi took out the other one alive. Rat took out his dead. Tiger got into a temper an' made a spring at Rat to catch him. Rat was running. The track was along the side of a wall. Anansi call, "Brer Pat, 'member stone-hole!" Tiger say, "What you say, Brer Nansi?" Anansi say, "Tell you mus' min', him go into dat stone-hole now!" Rat hear now, get into de stone-hole.

Tiger wheel roun' to revenge himself on Anansi. Anansi get under de dry trash. That is the reason why rat so fond of stone-hole, an' Anansi, always find him under dry trash an' rubbish.

Jack man dory!

Goat and Ananasi
by Ethel Watson, Santa Cruz Mountains

Anansi and Goat was walking one day. Dey met on Tiger nest. Dey saw seven pic'ny in de nes'. Hanansi said, "Goat, you know what we do? Mak we wring de neck t'row 'way in de bag!" Dey wring de pickney neck t'row it in de bag.

Dey met wid Bredder Tiger. Hanansi said, "Bredder Tiger, we get at' yo' nes' an' we tak yo' pic'ny an wring dem neck t'row 'em in de bag." Tiger say, "You mus' be kill me pic'ny!" Anansi say, "No-o-o-o-o!" Tiger say, "T'row 'em out let me see dem!"

Hanansi t'row out; dey didn't dead. "Goat, t'row out yours now let me see!" Goat Crow dem out; de Goat's was dead.

Tiger start after Goat. Hanansi say, "Run, Brer Tiger! run, Brer Goat!" Goat slip into a hole, Tiger begin to dig de hole. De stick get broke, Hanansi say, "Bredder Tiger, go look better stick." Bredder Tiger went. Hanansi give de Goat some salt, say, "When Tiger come, blow dis in a eye!" Tiger come back, begin to dig. Hanansi say, "Bredder Tiger, dig an peep down in a hole!"

Tiger begin dig an' peep. Goat blow de salt in de Tiger eye. Tiger say, "Brer Hanansi, blow in dis fe me!" Hanansi blow, say, "Bredder Tiger, after eye-water sweet so, what t'ink upon de meat?" Hanansi an' Goat come out an' kill Tiger, den dey put Tiger in de bag wid de pic'ny, an' bot' of dem went home.

New Names
by Samuel Christie, St, Ann's Bay

There was four friends; one was Anansi, name of the other was Tiger, name of the other Tacoomah, name of the other Parrot. So they go for a journey, and Anansi bargain with them that the four mus' change their name an' when they come home, each one mus' go to their mudder house an' if their mudder call them the old name they mus' eat their mudder.

So the new name,—Anansi name was Che-che-bun-da, Parrot new name was Green-corn-ero, Tiger name was Yellow-prissenda, Tacoomah name was Tacoomah-vengeance,—the four new name. Any mudder call them the ol' name, they mus' eat the mudder.

So they come to Tacoomah house first. Anansi say Tacoomah name 'Tacoomah-vengeance'. The mudder didn't understand the new name, so she say, "Look me pickney Tacoomah come!" An' kill Tacoomah mudder an' eat him. Second, 'em go to Tiger mudder. Anansi say Tiger name 'Yellow-prissenda'.

So they fall upon Tiger mudder, eat her. So that night Anansi cry to excuse the night an' go over to his mudder house an' say, "Mudder, if you call me Anansi', dey will kill you! but de name 'Che-che-bun-da'." The next night they come to Parrot house. Anansi say Parrot name 'Green-corn-ero'. Eat Parrot mudder the same.

At night, again Anansi cry excuse an' go to his mudder, say, "Mudder, las' night wha' me tell you say me name?" The mudder say, "Me pickney, you no name Anansi?" Anansi say, "Ma, coming here tomorrow night an' if you call me so they kill you!

You mus' call me 'Che-che-bun-da'!" Ask his mudder again, "Wha' me tell you say yo' pickney name?" She say, "Anansi?" Anansi say, "No, mudder! dey kill you! Me name Che-che-bun-da, Che-che-bun-da, Che-che-bun-da, Che-che-bun-da!" Keep tell the name over an' over that the mudder no forget.

So the night now Anansi turn come and they come along singing,
"Anansi name a Che-che-bun-da,
Cherry-senda, Yellow-prissenda,
Parrot name a Green-corn-ero,
Cherry-senda, Yellow-prissenda,
Tiger name a Yellow-prissenda,
Cherry-senda, Yellow-prissenda,
Tacoomah name Tacoomah-vengeance,
Cherry-senda, Yellow-prissenda."

An' as Anansi mudder see Anansi coming an' the rest, say, "Look me pickney Che-che-bun-da!" Call the new name, so her life save, an' didn't eat Anansi mudder. Anansi make the bargain to feast on the others an' save his mudder!

Long-Shirt
by Moses Hendricks, Mandeville

Anansi, Tacoomah and Tiger made a dance; Anansi was the fiddler, Tacoomah the drummer and Tiger the tambourine man. They travel on till they get to a country where all the people were naked—no clothing except the head-man, who wore a long shirt; he had a wooden leg. So they invite up all these people to come to the dance. Mr. Ram-goat was in the lot. So they start playing and the people start dancing, dance until they get so tired everybody fell asleep; and Anansi stole the head-man's shirt—good shirt!—and put his own old one upon him while he was sleeping.

The man got awake, miss his shirt. Now this shirt could talk. The man call out, "Long-shirt, whe' you deh?" Longshirt answer, "Brar Nansi have me on-o!" They start up, now. Anansi got so frightened! He met Brar Ram-goat. He said, "Brar Ram-goat, I swap me shirt, gi' you one new one fe you ol' one!" Ram-goat readily make the exchange. The head-man call out, "Long-shirt, whe' you deh?" Long-shirt call out, "Bra' Ram-goat have me on now-o!"

Ram-goat run until he was exhausted, couldn't go any further. He dug a hole an' bury himself into the, hole leaving one horn outside and didn't know that horn was projecting outside. The man with the wooden leg couldn't go as fast as the rest. All the rest ran past Ram-goat; the head-man came along, buck the wooden leg upon the horn and he fell down. When he got up, he thought it was a stump, so he got out his knife to cut off that stump to prevent it throwing him down again. He cut an' cut an' cut till he saw blood. He call out to the rest, "Look! come now-o, dirtee have blood!" All the rest come around say, "Dig him out! dig him out! dig him out!" After they dug him out, they took off head-man long shirt, put on his own old one, and they wet him with all the dirty slops—they drench poor Ramgoat.

They thought he was dead and they leave him an' go away. After they was gone, Ram-goat got up. He wring the dirty clothes, he wring with all the slop they throw on him; he never remember to wring his beard. Jack man dora! That's the reason the goat have such an offensive smell until this day, he didn't remember to wring his beard!

Shut Up in the Pot
by Simeon Falconer, Santa Cruz Mountains

There was a very hard time, no food whatsoever could they get, so Anansi him family well fear. So when Bredder Tiger and Bredder Tacoomah go see him, he tell them for last three or four days his wife and children didn't eat bread.

Say they will go back home and send him some of 'em food, and the two go back from Nansi yard and just dodge him now and hear his wife call, "Heah! dinner ready!" And Bredder Tiger and Bredder Tacoomah go back to the house knock on the door. The wife open the door and Anansi go right out of the house—'shamed! The wife give them some of the food to eat and it was only fresh beef.

They come back to Bredder Anansi now and Nansi tell them say, "I will get the beef, but whatever I tell you to do, you mus' be sure to do it." An' he put on a big pot of water on fire, an' him, Nansi, get into the pot of water and gwine tell them shut him up in him pot, An' tell them as soon as him knock the pot, open the pot.

An' him come out now, tell Bredder Tiger he mus' get in the pot,—Tacoomah long side in the pot too. And shut them up, an' he get a heavy weight an' put it on the pot top. An' he went right outside and tell him wife mus' shove up the fire, mak the fire bigger an' bigger. An' when him come back, them was properly cooked.

They gwine eat now, he was tuning up his fiddle—

"I got them now! I got them now!

Them think they got me, but I got them now!"

Tracking Anansi
by Simeon Falconer, Santa Cruz Mountains

Anansi live into a tree with wife and children, then go about and robber the others and they can't find where he live. So Tiger and Bredder Tacoomah dog him and see when he send down the rope and swing up whatever he provide for the family. So Bredder Tiger go to a tin-smith to give him a fine v'ice and went to the tree and him sing,

"Mama, mama, sen' down rope,
Sen' down rope, Brer Nansi deh groun' a!"

Then the mother find out it was not Bredder Nansi from the coarseness of the v'ice. So he go to a gold-smith now and he come back again and sing again. Now he get a v'ice same as Bredder Nansi.

"Mama, mama, sen' down rope,
Sen' down rope, Brer Nansi deh groun' a!"
Then the mother let the rope down to receive him. Brer Nansi coming from a distance see the mother swinging him up in the tree now and say,

"Mama, cut de rope! mama, cut de rope!"

And she cut the rope and Bredder Tiger fell and broke his neck. Bredder Nansi tak him and have him now for him dinner. They couldn't eat Bredder Nansi at all; him was the smartest one of all.

Rabbit and Children Goin' Up to Heaven by William Sounders, Mandeville

Once de Rabbit an' chil'ren was going up to Heaven. Dey was singin' dat dey goin' up to Heaven t'-day, an' Brar Anansi want to go along wid dem to have a feed. Having got in de merit dey sing,

"Mammy an' Harry,

Pull up de merit, pull up de merit!"

An' when Anansi quite away on de journey was goin' up to heaven, he was singin',

"Pull up de merit, pull up de merit!"

An' de Rabbits say, "What is dat? Dat is Anansi voice!"

De chil'ren say, "Yes, dat is Anansi voice." Rabbits say,

"Mammy an' Harry,

Cut down de merit, cut down de merit!"

An' de merit cut down an' from dat day poor Anansi's waist was cut off, leave a little bit!

Goat on the Hill Side
by Julia Gentle, Santa Cruz Mountains

The time hard. Anansi said to Tacoomah, "How going to manage wid de hard time?" So Tacoomah said, "You know we do? I will get me machete an' I go half shut de door, den I will say, 'Police, I sick!'"

Den, when people come, Tacoomah take de machete an' chop dem, put dem in de barrel for de hungry time. Anansi say, "Brar Tacoomah, barrel nearly full?"—"No, Brar." He cry out again how Tacoomah poorly; an' de people come an' as dey come, he kill dem put in barrel to serve in hungry time.

Den Goat up on de hill-side say he see everybody goin' in, nobody come out; de house so little, how is it gwine to hold all doze people?

So Goat come down now off de hill-side to see how Tacoomah. He peep in. Tacoomah say, "Come in!" an' Goat run right back up hill-side. An' from dat day, Goat stay up on hill-side.

Tacoomah's Corn Piece
by Adolphus Iron, Claremont, St. Ann

Tacoomah plant a piece of corn. When it commence to dry, den begin to t'ief it. Tacoomah charge Hanansi. Hanansi say, "Brar, no me!"

By dis time Hanansi was a fiddler. Hanansi tell Tacoomah say, "Brar, you say me broke you' corn, you mek one dance an' get me fe play." Tacoomah say yes.

De night of de dance, Hanansi get one gang tell dem say, "As you hear me begin play, you start a-brekkin'." De tune Hanansi play was dis fe de whole night:

"Two two grain, broke dem go 'long,
Eb'rybody broke, broke dem go 'long,
Green an' dry, broke dem go 'long."

In de morning when de dance finish, Tacoomah go down a him cornpiece. Him holla out, "Lawd! Brar Nansi, come heah! not one lef'."

Hanansi turn 'roun' say, "T'ink you say a me a t'ief you corn. Las' night you no get me fe play a you dance? den if dem broke out you corn, how you say a me?"

Tacoomah tak it to heart an' drop down dead.

Anansi and the Tar Baby
by George Parkes, Mandeville

Tacoomah is Anansi friend an' neighbor, live very near in one house but different apartment, so whenever one talk the other can hear. Anansi an' Tacoomah both of them work groun' together at one place. Anansi don't wait upon his food till it is ripe, but dig out an' eat it. Tacoomah wait until it fit to eat it. After Anansi eat off his own, he turn to Tacoomah an' begin to t'ief it. Every morning Tacoomah go, he find his groun' mashed up. He said, "Brar Nansi, tak care a no you deh mash up me groun' a nighttime!" Anansi said, "No-o, Brar, but if you t'ink dat a me deh t'ief a yo' groun' a nighttime, you call me t'-night see if me no 'peak to you."

Tacoomah went to his groun' and get some tar an' tar a 'tump an' lef' it in de center of de groun'. Now night come, Anansi get a gourd, fill it wid water, bore a hole underneat' de gourd jus' as much as de water can drop tip, tip, tip. He cut a banana-leaf an' put it underneat' de gourd so de water could drop on it. After dey bot' went to bed, every now and again Tacoomah called out and Anansi say, "Eh!" Afterward Anansi say, "Me tired fe say 'eh', me wi' say 'tip'." So Anansi put de gourd of water up on a stand wid de banana-leaf underneat', so when Tacoomah say, "Anansi?" de water drop "tip." An' at dis time Anansi gone to de groun'.

He saw de black 'tump which Tacoomah tar an' lef' in de groun'. So Anansi open his right han' an' box de 'tump. His right han' fasten. He said to de 'tump, "If you no let me go I box you wid de lef' han'!" He box him wid de lef', so bot' han' fasten now. He say now, "Den you hol' me two han'? If you not le' me go I kick you!" He then kick the 'tump an' the right foot fasten first. He kick it with the lef' foot an' the lef' foot fasten too. He say, "Now you hol' me two han' an' me two foot! I gwine to buck you if you don' le' go me han' an' foot!" He den buck de 'tump an' his whole body now fasten on de 'tump. He was deh for some minutes. He see Goat was passing. He said, "Brar Goat, you come heah see if you kyan't more 'an we t'-day." So Goat come. Anansi say, "Brar Goat, you buck him!" Goat buck de 'tump; Anansi head come off an' Goat head fasten. He said, "Brar Goat, you kick him wid you two foot!" An' Goat kick him an' Anansi two han' come off an' Goat two foot fasten. He said, "Brar Goat, now you push him!" Goat push him, an' Anansi two foot come off an' Anansi free an' Goat fasten. So Anansi go back home an' say to Tacoomah, "Me tired fe say 'tip', now; me wi' say 'eh'."

In de morning, bot' of dem went to groun'. Anansi say, "Brar Tacoomah, look de fellah deh t'ief yo' groun', dat fe' a Goat!" Goat say, "No, Brar Tacoomah, Anansi lirs' fasten on de 'tump heah an' he ask me fe buck him off!" Anansi say, "A yaie,[1] sah!" an' say, "Brar Tacoomah, no me an' you sleep fe de whole night an' ev'ry time yo' call me, me 'peak to you?" Tacoomah say yes. He say Tacoomah, "Mak we ki' de fallah Goat!" So dey kill Goat an' carry him home go an' eat him.

The Grave
by Stanley Jones, Claremont, St. Ann

Once Mrs. Anansi had a large field. She planted it with peas. Anansi was so lazy he would never do any work. He was afraid that they would give him none of the peas, so he pretended to be sick. After about nine days, he called his wife an' children an' bid them farewell, tell them that he was about to die, an' he ask them this last request, that they bury him in the mids' of the peas-walk, but firs' they mus' make a hole thru the head of the coffin an' also in the grave so that he could watch the peas for them while he was lying there. An' one thing more, he said, he would like them to put a pot and a little water there at the head of the grave to scare the thieves away. So he died and was buried.

All this time he was only pretending to be dead, an' every night at twelve o'clock he creep out of the grave, pick a bundle of peas, boil it, and after having a good meal, go back in the grave to rest. Mistress Anansi was surprised to see all her peas being stolen. She could catch the thief no-how. One day her eldest son said to her, "Mother, I bet you it's my father stealing those peas!" At that Mrs. Anansi got into a temper, said, "How could you expect your dead father to rob the peas!" Said, "Well, mother, I soon prove it to you." He got some tar an' he painted a stump at the head of the grave an' he put a hat on it.

When Anansi came out to have his feast as usual, he saw this thing standing in the groun'. He said, "Good-evening, sir!" got no

reply. Again he said, "Good-evening, sir!" an' still no reply. "If you don' speak to me I'll kick you!" He raise his foot an' kick the stump an' the tar held it there like glue. "Let me go, let me go, sir, or I'll knock you down with my right hand!" That hand stuck fast all the same. I'll you don' let me go, I'll hit you with my lef' hand!" That hand stick fas' all the same. An' he raise his lef' foot an' gave the stump a terrible blow. That foot stuck. Anansi was suspended in air an' had to remain there till morning. Anansi was so ashamed that he climb up beneath the rafters an' there he is to this day.

The Dunko Tree
by William Forbes,
Dry River, Cock-pit Country

Deh was Anansi.—Tacoomah was Anansi son. Den was a hard time. Anansi had a Duckano tree had some Duckano on it. An' he had t'ree pickney; when he go out a night, eat him belly full, come back carry 'em a bag. Now when him wife mak a little dinner fe him, tell him no, he don' want it, gi' it to pickney dem. Tacoomah tell mama cut little hole in Anansi trab'ling bag an' t'row ashes in it.

Fast as he go 'long, ashes drop straight to de Duckano tree. Den Tacoomah follow de ashes till him fin' out de Duckano tree. An' when him fetch to de Duckano tree, pick off all, lef' one; an' him tell de Duckano, "As Anansi come fe pick you, drop a dirt!" An' as de Duckano drop a dirt, Anansi say, "Yes, dat de bes' place I want you fe go!"

Come down to pick him up, Duckano go back on tree. Anansi say, "Cho! dat de bes' place I pick you t'-day". Go back on tree, couldn't catch it. An' not a creature can pick de Duckano, but Tacoomah!

Den, as Anansi go up de Duckano tree, him see Dog a come. An' said, "Brar Dog, go pick up Duckano fe me!" an' as de Duckano drop, dog come pickee up; den, as Dog pick him up, Dog nyam de Duckano.

Dog run 'round so, Anansi go after him so. Dog go into one deep hole, jus' two eye look out a deh. Little out de two eye, Anansi pass an' see him, draw him out of de hole an' 'queeze out de Duckano. Wha' mak de two sink place in Dog side, Anansi 'queeze out Duckano.

Jack man dora!

The Handsome Packey
by Moses Hendricks, Mandeville

Once the times was very hard. So Anansi had a wife an' six children dependent on him; wherever he goes he gets something, so he gets seven plantains, one apiece. His wife said to him, "Where is yours?" Said 'he mustn't mind him; when they coo it, each one mus' give him piece-piece. At the end he got more than anyone 'cause he got seven pieces.

He went out another day in search of food and he saw a calabash tree with one calabash on it, an' he look at it an' said, "My! there's a han'some packey!" The packey say, "I han'some an' I can do han'some work." He said, "Do it let I see!" Packey put a table before him full of nice eatables; when he eat to his satisfaction, packey shut up everything.

He took the packey home with him an' he shut it up in his loft over-head. Every day he hide from the family an' go up there have his good feed an' whatever little rubbish he bring in, he give it to them. His wife an' children watch him an' fin' what he have.

After he was gone out, they play the same game—"What a han'some packey!"—"I han'some an' can do han'some work."—"Do it let we see!"—They carelessly let the packey drop from them an' crack. When Anansi go home, go to his feed, say, "What a han'some packey!" packey don't give him any answer. He find that something was wrong.

Went out another day an' saw another packey (which was the same packey), says, "There's a han'some packey!" Packey said, "I han'some an' can do han'some work." He said, "Do it let I see!" Packey took out a cow-whip an' give him a handsome flogging. He t'ought of having a good joke on the family an' pick it an' hung it up in the loft upon the same place.

So the wife an' chil'ren went to this packey again, expecting the same thing; so the wife said, "There's a han'some packey!" Packey said, "I han'some an' I can do han'some work!" The six chil'ren were around the packey.

The wife said, "Do it let we see!" and the packey out with the, cow-whip an' fall in to lash them right an' left. Some tumble down, some get into the shingle hide themselves all around in the crevice. Jack man dora! That's the reason why you see Anansi live in the crevice!

The Knife and Fork
by William Forbes,
Dry River, Cock-pit Country

Anansi was cutting a ground 'gainst a ribber-side an' he had a hatchet an' de hatchet get 'way from him into de sea. An' him pull off him clo'es go dive fe de hatchet an' in'tead of fin' de hatchet him fin' a knife an' fo'k.

An' when him come home, he put knife an' fo'k 'pon table an' say, "Lay out, knife an' fo'k, lay out!" An' it lay out anyt'ing he ax fe. Well, den, him get a party, lots of people into de house to show dem what knife an' fo'k can do. An' after de people come into de house, he put dem knife an' fo'k on de table an' say, "Lay out, me knife an' fo'k, lay out!" An' all de people eat.

An' ants mak nest 'pon de knife an' fo'k now. Well, den, nex' day mo'ning when he tak out knife an' fo'k, say, "Lay out, me knife an' fo' kill not'ing at all come out. It spoil!

Well, him go back to de ribber-side wid anudder hatchet an' was chopping, fling away in de sea. An' after him dive, dive an' fin' a horse-whip in de sea. An' as he go home say, "Lay out, horse-whip, lay out mak a eat!" An' de horse-whip lay out an' flog him, wattle him well till he holla.

An' he only sen' back fe all doze people who eat wid de knife an' fo'k, say he going to mak a great dinner an' all de people mus' come. An' when de people dem come, he put dem into de house an' tak out his chil'ren an' wife, put a kitchen.

An' put de horse-whip on de table an' lock up de windeh, say if do' an windeh open can not get dinner. An' he tell de horse-whip mus' lay out mak dem eat. An' de horse-whip flog dem all till dey break down de house.

Anansi is a man nobody can fool him—only Brar Dead!"

The Riddle
by Moses Hendricks, Mandeville

Tacoomah and Anansi were great friends. Tacoomah got into trouble. He was tried and sentenced to be hung. Anansi said, "Brer Tacoomah, no fret! I'm a good liar; I play you off." Anansi went to the king to beg for Tacoomah. The king said to him, "If you give me a puzzle that I can't answer, I will let him off."

Anansi went home. Tacoomah had a mare that was heavy with colt. He said, "Brer Tacoomah, if you do as I tell you, I can get you off." Tacoomah said, "Brer Nansi, I will do anything to save me life!"

Go for the mare—the one heavy with colt—open the mare's stomach and took out the colt, then took a bit of the mare's skin and cut out a bridle. Then Tacoomah got some fresh dirt and filled his hat and put it on, got some silver and put it into one boot and throw some gold into the other boot. Next, Tacoomah mount the colt.

Anansi said, "Come now, Brer Tacoomah, go now and see king." He told Tacoomah all that he was to say to the king when he met him; Anansi put him up to all the talk.

They said to the king:
"Under the earth I stood,
Silver and gold was my tread,

I rode a thing that never was born,
An' a bit of the dam I hold in me hand."

The king couldn't guess it; he said, "You must explain to my satisfaction." And he said, "I have me hat full of dirt" (took off his hat and show him), "one boot with silver" (he was standing on silver), "the other boot with gold" (he was standing on gold also). He rode "a colt that was never born" (he cut that out of the mother's belly), and "a bit of the dam" he held in his hand—that was the mare's skin he had as a bridle.

The king reprimanded him and said, "Go on, me good man, go about your business!"

Jack man dory! Anansi got him off, Anansi was a smart man!

Filing a Mile
by George Parkes, Mandeville

Anansi one day went to a river to catch fish, an' while fishin' down the stream, he came across a hole. He put his han' down in the hole an' something hol' the han'. He said, "A who hol' me?" The something said, "No me!"—"Me who?" The thing said, "No me Fling-a-mile!" Anansi said, "Fling me a mile mak I see." The t'ing wheel Anansi, wheel him, an' fling him one mile from the spot. When Anansi drop, he nearly knock out his senses.

He said, "I mus' eat somet'ing out of dat hole!" He went an' get six iron fork an' six wooden one an' stick up at the place where he drop. Nex' day he was going back down fe fishing. He meet up Hog. He said, "Bredder Hog, mak we go down a river go ketch fish now?" Hog said yes. When they reach the river, both of them started. Anansi, he walk on the side where the hole are not, Hog, he walk on the side where the hole are. Anansi look over to Hog way and said, "What a pretty hole in front of Bredder Hog deh! You mus' get somet'ing out of de hole deh. I don' min' if it befo' me!" So Anansi tell Hog to put his han' in the hole see if him feel anyt'ing. Hog put in him han'. Hog said, "Somet'ing hol' me han'!" Anansi said, "Ax a who hol' you!" Hog said, "A who hol' me?" The t'ing say, "A me!" Anansi say, "Ax him, say 'A me who?'" Hog say, "A me who?" The t'ing say, "No me Fling-a-mile!" Anansi said to Hog, "Tell him fling you a mile mak you see." Hog say, "Fling me a mile mak I see!" The t'ing wheel Hog, wheel him, wheel him, drop him right on the fork

Anansi fix up. Hog drop dead. Anansi tak up Hog put him in a bag and said, "I well wan' fe eat you long time!" At that time Monkey was on the tree watching Anansi.

The nex' day Anansi start back to the river, meet up Bredder Goat. He say, "Bredder Goat, mak we go down a river, go ketch fish?" Goat say yes. Anansi tol' Goat to walk on the hand where the hole is an' he walk on the opposite side. While going along Anansi said, "What a pretty hole in front of Br'er Goat deh! You mus' fin' somet'ing in a hole like dat. I wish it were me de hole we' deh befo'!" Anansi said to Goat, "Put yo' han' in deh see if you can fin' anyt'ing." Goat put the han' in the hole. Somet'ing hol' him. He said, "Somet'ing hol' me!" Anansi said, "Ax a who hol' you!" Goat said, "A who hol' me?" The t'ing said, "No me!" Anansi said, "Ax 'A me who?'" Goat say, "A me who?" The t'ing say, "No me Fling-a-mile." Anansi said, "Tell him fling you a mile mak you see!" Goat say, "Fling me a mile mak I see!" He wheel Goat, whee' whee' wheel, an' drop him right on the fork one mile. Goat drop dead. Anansi took up Goat an' put him in his bag, said, "I well wan' you fe eat a long time!" At that time Monkey was still watching him.

The nex' day he start to go out again; he met up Br'er Dog. Anansi said to Dog, "Mak we go down a river go ketch fish!" Dog say yes. On reaching to the river, Anansi tell Dog to walk on the side where the hole is an' he walk on the opposite side. On reaching to the hole Anansi said, "What a pretty hole in front of Br'er Dog! You mus' fin' somet'ing in dat hole. I wish it we' deh befo' me!" Anansi say to Dog, "Put yo' ban' in deh if you feel anyt'ing." Dog put the han' in the hole. Something hol' him. He said to Anansi, "Somet'ing hol' me!" Anansi said, "Ax 'A who hol' me?'" Dog said, "A who hol' me?" The somet'ing say, "No me!" Anansi say, "Ax him 'me who?'" Dog say, "Me who?" The somet'ing say, "No me Fling-a-mile!" Anansi say, "Tell him fling you a mile mak you see!" Dog said, "Fling me a mile mak me see!" The t'ing fling Dog whee'-a, whee'-a, whee', an' dash him one mile on the stake. Dog drop on the stake dead. Anansi tak up Dog, put him in his bag an' said, "A well wan' you fe eat long time!"

Now Monkey couldn't bear it no longer, come off the tree. The nex' day while Anansi was going down, Monkey put himself in the way where Anansi was to meet him. Anansi said, "Br'er Monkey, mak we go down a river go ketch fish." Monkey say, "Yes, a well wan' company fe go down too!" On reaching to the river, Monkey walk on the side where the hole is an' Anansi on the opposite side. On reaching to the hole Anansi said, "What a pretty hole in front of Br'er Monkey! You mus' fin' somet'ing in a hole like a dat. I wish a we' me i' deh befo'!" Anansi said to Monkey, "Put yo' han' in deh, see if you fin' anyt'ing." Monkey say, "No, Br'er, me go put me han' in deh, somet'ing go hol' me!" Anansi said, "No, man, me no t'ink not'ing wi' hol' you!" Monkey said, "You come put yo' han' in deah." Anansi said, "No, as you de closee, you put fe you han' in deah." Monkey said, "No! somet'ing wi' hol' me!"—"No! not'ing no in deah fe hol' you!" So Anansi go near to the hole now and tell Monkey mus' put down him han', an' Monkey refuse. Anansi now make attempt to put his han',—like that—in the hole, an' Monkey push it down, an' the somet'ing hol' Anansi han' now. Monkey said to Anansi, "Tak out de han'!" Anansi say, "Me han' kyan' come out; somet'ing hol' it!" Monkey says, "Ask a who hol' you." Anansi speak in a very feeble v'ice, say, "A who hol' me?" The t'ing say, "No me!" Monkey say to Anansi, "Ax' A me who.'" Anansi said in a feeble tone of v'ice all 'e time, "A me who?" The t'ing say, "A me Fling-a-mile." Monkey say, "Tell him fe fling you a mile mak you see." Anansi now said in a feeble tone of v'ice, "Fling me a mile mak I see!" So tak Anansi an' wheel him, whee', whee'! An' while it was wheeling him he said to Monkey, "Br'er Monkey, run one mile from heah, whe' you see some iron an' wooden fork,—jus' haul dem out fe me!" Monkey tak off him hat an' run half way an' stop where he could see when Anansi drop. Anansi drop on de fork an' belly burst 'tiff dead! An' Monkey take him an' put him in his bag, take him go eat him.

Horse and Anansi
by Alexander Archibald, Mandeville

Anansi call Horse a go bush cut plantain. When dey cut done, dey carry out in de open, dey begin to play stick, lick stick. Den Anansi said, "Brar Horse, we hungry now, we don' have no fire fe roast plantain."

So say to Horse, "Go see fire quite yonder? Go deh, go tak fire come, mak we roast plantain!" Horse fling up him tail on back, gallop, gone. Meanwhile him gone, Anansi 'trike him tinder-box an buil' a fire roast every plantain; eat all de plantain, leave only four. Horse gallop away an' kyan' ketch de fire an' turn back.

Anansi say, "Brar Horse, when you gone, one man pass heah gi' me fire an' me roast de plantain; as me roas'ee done, one man come beat me an' tak away de plantain on'y lef' dem four heah gi' me!" So Brar Horse say, "Never min'! you tak two, me tak two." So Horse takee.

Dat time Brar Goat go bush kneel down watch Brar Anansi, watch what take place; so de nex' day, Goat say him will go wid Anansi. Dem two go, dem two cut plantain, an' dem come out 'pon de open an' dem play.

So Anansi said, "Brar Goat, we hungry now an' we ha' no fire. See fire quite yonder? gallop go get fire an' come." Goat gallop, go roun' clump of bush, go kneel down on knee go watch him. Him 'trike him tinder-box mak a fire, peel ev'ry plantain put a fire.

When de plantain roast, he 'crape ev'ry bit. As him 'crapee, Goat get up a come. Goat cut 'tick an' him jump one side so him put circle roun' de fire-side, an' say to Anansi, "Put you han' in now, sah!" an' jump de odder side an' put circle again. So den Anansi begin to beg, an' Goat tak away eberyt'ing didn't gib him one!

Jack man dory!

Anansi in Monkey Country
by Elizabeth Hilton,
Harmony Hall, Cock-pit Country

Anansi go to Monkey country. Put on a big pot of water an' tell the Monkey when him get in the pot of water, when him say "Bunya", they mus' take him out of the pot of water. When they take him out, they mus' go in.

So when he go in the pot of water, as soon as he feel the water hot he say, "Bunya." They take him out. An' put all of them one time into the pot of water. An' when them said, "Bunya!" Anansi said, "No bunya yet!" An' said, "Bunya!" Anansi said, "No bunya yet!" Anansi wouldn't take them out until them boil. Anansi take them out an' eat them.

One little one let' at the top of the pot that the water didn't scald. That one run go to the next Monkey country an' tell them the story about Anansi an' the 'bunya.' When Anansi eat, he start to the other country, an' him go there an' tell the Monkey mus' put him into the pot of water an' when he say, "Bunya," mus' take him out.

So when Anansi feel the water hot, he say, "Bunya!" Monkey say, "No bunya yet!" Anansi say, "Bunya!" Monkey say, "No bunya yet!" Monkey keep Anansi in that pot till him kill him.

The Fishes
by Rennie Macfarlane, Mandeville

Three little fish pickney mother was sick an' Anansi said, "If you want, I get you' mother better for you!" an the three little fish said, "Yes!" An' said, "You give me a frying-pan an' some sweet ile, an' you lock up in that room an' when she better, I let you know." An' he fry the fish an' eat it an' tell the fish pickney that they can come out the room now. An' they ask, "Where is our mother? Did you get her better?" an' he said, "No, I eat her!" an' the fish run after him an' he run away.

An' a mule ask the fish, "Do you want me to catch him for you?" an' they said, "Yes!" And the mule said, "Give me those peas that you have now an' I catch him for you." An' the mule go out to Anansi gate an' lie down there an' when Anansi come out, Anansi run up into his belly an' the mule gallop away again. An' Anansi cry out in the mule's belly, "If he go to sea-side, stop him; but if he go anywhere else, let him go!" An' he gallop to the sea-shore an' give Anansi to the fish.

An' he say, "You know what you do, fish? Put me under the trash an' burn me!" An' when the fish put him under de trash, Anansi run under a stone, hide, an' the fish t'ot he was burn.

Anansi, White-belly and Fish
by Mrs. Ramtalli, Maggotty

Anansi is accustomed to lie in the sun every morning watching the birds going to feed. One day he said to White-belly, "Brar White-belly, whe' you go to feed eb'ry day? tek me wid you." So White-belly promised on condition that he would behave himself. He fitted him out with a pair of wings to fly, and they went to the feeding-trees. These overhung a river. Every tree White-belly went on, Anansi said, "A fe me tree dat!" and White-belly went away to another. Anansi eat so much that he fell fast asleep. White-belly got annoyed. When Anansi was sleeping, he went and took off the false wings. Anansi turned in his sleep and fell into the river.

The Fish picked him up and took him to their home. He said, "Cousin Fish, no eat me!"—"If we are 'cousin' we wi' see!" Fish boiled some hot rice-pop. Anansi said, "It no hot enough! putee in the sun mekee hot more!" When he thought is was quite cooled off, put it to his head, never stopped drinking until it was finished. Then Fish say, "Yes, me cousin fe trew!"

It was getting night and Fish told him to remain over until next day. Fish had a barrel of eggs in the kitchen. Anansi wanted to eat them off, asked Fish to make his bed in the kitchen for the night. He poached all the eggs in the ashes, left one, and they went 'pop!' The pickney say, "A wha' stranger man a do deh?" The Fish mother said, "Have manners, pickney! Let you cousin prosper." Morning dawn, the mother sent the children to bring the eggs to her to count them. Anansi said, "Mek the child'ren keep quiet; me wi' work!" and he took the one egg, took it to the mother Fish. Each time she marked it he would wipe it off, take back the same egg, until he had taken the whole barrel full.

After that, he said he wanted to go. Fish said to two of the children, "Me son, get the canoe an' tek you cousin over the river." It was looking very breezy and rainy. When they got half way across, Fish bawled out at the top of her voice, "Bring stranger man back he-e-ah! fe he eat off all me eggs; only one is heah!" The children say, "Wha' ma say?" Anansi said, "You ma say you mus' row quickly, squall ahead!" The children rowed across. Anansi took them up, put them in his bag and took them home, eat them. And from that day, fishes are eaten!

Goats Escape
by Richard Pottinger, Claremont, St. Ann

Anansi and Goat have a little quarrel. Anansi said to Goat, 'Brar Goat, I gwine ketch you!" Goat say, "You never live, me frien', to ketch me!" Goat 'fraid fe rain. So one moist night Goat was coming from his field had to pass Anansi's house, drizzle drizzle rain fall; Brar Goat have to run up Anansi's house.—"Come in, me frien'!" Goat go in.

Anansi step in a room tak out him fiddle: —
"Me t'ank Brar Rain
Fe run wil' meat from bush
Come a house."

Goat didn't like it, keep to de door-way. Anansi not notice him, only playing de same song, Goat jump down de bottom door Anansi cut after him. Goat can't cross river, run to de river-side turn a white little stone. Dog see, de odder side of de river, when Goat turned a little stone. Anansi run up de river now.—"Brar Dog, see Brar Goat pass?"—"Yes, Brar! see one little stone a riverside deh? takee up t'rowee, I show you whe' him deh." Anansi tak up de stone, t'row it de odder side, give Brar Dog. Goat drop on him four feet. Anansi say, "Luck in me han' an' it get 'way!"

The Dance
by Elizabeth Hilton,
Harmony Hall, Cock-pit Country

Assono an' Anansi make a dance and invite Goat and Dog to the dance. Anansi make bargain with Assono that when Goat an' Dog come in, he mus' sit down at one door an' Anansi at the other.

Assono sing, (repeat three times)—
"I sit down a me house deh fe dey come!"

So Anansi sing,
"Whe' me been tell you!"

Dog sing,
"The somebody kyan't run, you no hearie?"

Goat sing,
'I kyan't run, but I cunnie do!"

Anansi say to him, "Brar Goat, you no play de fiddle good! mak me tak de fiddle stan' 'pon de do'mat play better." That time he gone to shut the door, Dog and Goat run thru' the other door before Assono catch them. Assono an' Anansi run after them an' get to a big river.

Dog can swim an' Goat kyan't swim, so Dog swim over the river an' lef' Goat. Goat turn a big rock an' lie by the roadside. Dog say to

Anansi, "Brar Anansi, tak a rock-stone, lick me down an' I wi' stay mak you come pick me up!" Anansi tak a big rock so an' fling over the river. Goat get up an' holla "Baa-a-a-a!" Assono so vex with Anansi that he eat him up same place.

Hanansi Give a Dance
by Alfred Williams, Maroon Town

Hanansi give a dance, invite any amount of company, an', de night, everbody come. He invite Brar Goat, an' when him come, Brar Goat stay outside on de landing, an' Brar Hanansi inside say him gwine to play, an' he play,

Meat a da me yard, Meat, come see me. Meat a da me yard, Meat, come see me.

Meat a da me yard, Meat, come see me. Meat a da me yard, Meat, come see me.

Brar Goat den dance. When he dance he holla,

You no have-y a han' you no sure of it,
You no have-y a han' you no sure of it,
You no have-y a han' you no sure of it,
You no have-y a han' you no sure of it.

Turtle's Escape
by Henry Spence, Bog, Westmoreland

Turtle fool Anansi one day. Anansi go out one day an' him catch one turtle,—quite glad of de turtle! So when he go home, Turtle know Anansi gwine eat him an' said to Anansi, "Brat Anansi, you know me fat?

When you put me on, as de water boil up you tak me off, 'cause fat will mash." So when de water get warm, him blow him nose mak de water boil up.

Anansi get frightened, said de turtle wi' mash! So he lay him down at de pan-side let de fat cool so him no mash, Turtle run away in de pond.

Anansi lose him dinner.

Fire and Anansi
by Henry Spence, Bog, Westmoreland

Anansi an' Fire were good frien'. So Anansi come an' see Fire an' dey had dinner. So he invite Fire fe come see him now. So Fire tell him he kyan't walk, So Fire tell him from him house him mus' lay path dry bush, an' him walk on top of dry bush.

Anansi married to Ground Dove. Ground Dove tell him no, he mustn't invite Fire; him wi' bu'n him house an' bu'n out himself. Anansi wouldn't hear what him wife say, an' he laid de trash on. An' Fire bu'n from him house, an' when he come near Anansi house he mak a big jump, bu'n Anansi, bu'n him house, bu'n eb'ryt'ing but him wife.

Fire fool Anansi!

Tailors and Fiddlers
by David Roach, Lacovia

Anansi and Lizard go to a ball. Anansi is a fiddler, Lizard is a tailor. Quit-quit was the fiddler.

Anansi was playing, "tum, tum, tum" and all the girls were going round Brar Quit-quit. So

Anansi play, "Me nyam-nyam taya!" an' it please the people. All love taya; all the girls crowded round Brar Anansi. Brar Quit-quit says, "Taya no somet'ing!" Then Anansi comes in with his music—"Me nyam de somet'ing! If taya no somet'ing, whe' are de somet'ing?"

Brar Anansi said mus' mak a suit of clo'es for him that kyan't match. Brar Quit-quit tell him mus' mak a suit out of maggot-fly. An' after the ball they went to dinner an' when the maggot-fly smell the meat, they run off leave him naked.

Fiddlers
by Henry Spence, Bog, Westmoreland

Anansi and Tiger bot' of dem are fiddler an' go play fe de king ball. So Tiger could play more dan Anansi. So de king say de man could play de best would get married to de king daughter. Dem had dinner after de ball, so after dem play, play, play, Anansi find Tiger playing more dan him, so de lady more cleave to Tiger. So Anansi whisper to Tiger, say Tiger mus' play,

Nyam nyam no not'ing!

As he commence play, de lady say de meaning "Belly-feed no not'ing, but mus' somet'ing!" So Anansi set him fiddle, play,

Bittle no somet'ing, what is somet'ing?

De lady cleave to Anansi an' drive away Tiger.

Spider Marries Monkey's Daughter
by May Ford, Newmarket

Bredder Monkey had a daughter whom Bredder Spider wanted to marry. Monkey didn't want Bredder Spider to marry his daughter as he thought Bredder Spider was too fast and beneath him; he only kept Bredder Spider company as he thought him useful to him, So he jump to Bredder Green-lizard and said, "Bredder Green-lizard, what you think of such cheek? Fancy! Bredder Spider want to marry me daughter! I don't want to hurt his feelings as he is useful to us, so help me to get out of it."

So Bredder Green-Lizard say, "I tell you a way, man. Call her 'Miss Nennan-kennan-wid-a-turn-down-gown' and whoever guess her name marry her, for Bredder Spider never can guess that!" So Bredder Lizard went direc' an' tell Bredder Spider, "When dey call you all up to ax Bredder Monkey daughter name, you fe say, 'Miss Nennen-kennen-wid-a-turn-down-gown'." So Bredder Monkey send out word to all the gentlemen who want to marry his daughter to come and guess her name. Not one could tell her name till when he catch to Bredder Spider, Bredder Spider say,

"Miss Nennen-kennen-wid-a-turn-down-gown." So Bredder Spider got Bredder Monkey daughter an' marry her.

So when Bredder Spider wife had a baby, she left Bredder Spider put the pickney to bed while she go to pond. When Bredder Spider think wife gone, him start to sing,

"Hush, me pickney, hush me baby,
A me cunnie mak me get yo' mama!"

Spider wife turn back an' say, "A what a dat you sing?" Spider say, 'Me only sing,
'Hush, me pickney! hush, me baby!

It's a good t'ing marry yo' mama?'"

Bredder Monkey been a come see him an' hear what Bredder Spider singing. Bredder Monkey say, "Wa' so you get me daughter!" an' grab away the baby an' kill Spider. And as him kill Spider the pickney drop out his hand dead.

So never kill a Spider, as whatever you have in hand will be sure to break.

The Chain of Victims
by Richard Morgan, Santa Cruz Mountains

Hanansi saw Brar Hog an' said, "Brar Hog, lend me a dollar, to-morrow, twelve o'clock, come fe it." An' saw Brar Dog an' said, "Brar Dog, len' me a dollar, to-morrow, twelve o'clock, come fe it." An' saw Brar Monkey an' say, "Brar Monkey, len' me a dollar, to-morrow, twelve o'clock, come fe it." An' saw Brar Tiger an' said, "Brar Tiger, len' me a dollar, to-morrow, twelve o'clock, come fe it. An saw Brar Lion an' say, "Len' me a dollar, to-morrow, twelve o'clock, come fe it."

Nex' day hear some one knock at de door. Hanansi said, "Who come deah?"—"Me, Brar Hog." An' he say, "Come in." He an' Hog stay dere talkin' an' hear anodder knockin'. An' say, "Who come deah?"—"Me, Brar Dog." He say, "Brar Hog, you run go in dat room, fe Dog too bad; if him catch you him are goin' to kill you!" Dog come in. Him stay dere talkin' until hear anodder knock an' said, "Who come deah?"—"Me, Brar Monkey." An' say, "Come in"; an' say, "Brar Dog, you run go in dat room dere an' when you go you see Brar Hog un'er de bed, kill him." Him an' Monkey talk till Tiger come knock at de door, an' Hanansi say, "Who knock deah?"—"Me, Brar Tiger." An' say, "Brar Monkey, run go in dat room hide or Tiger ketch you!" When Brar Tiger come in, him an' Hanansi deh talkin' till he hear annodder knock. An' say, "Who come deah?"—"Brar Lion." An' say, "Brar Tiger, you run go in dat room deh; you see Brar Monkey, kill him!"

So as Lion come in he tell Brar Lion, "Look heah! have plenty o' meat. Brar Tiger gone in dere; you gwine go kill him!" Lion went in an' kill Tiger. Me'while de Lion kill Tiger, Hanansi go out de kitchen door dig one deep hole an' ca' say, "Brar Lion, run come heah! We go put on little hot water fe clean up doze fellah!" As Lion jump out of de house, feel so glad, gallop on to de kitchen, he got down in de hole an bre'k his neck. So Hanansi said, "You brute! look how much money I borrow from you, an' I have all yo' bone to crack t'-night!"

Why Tumble Bug Rolls in the Dung
by William Forbes,
Dry River, Cock-pit Country

Deh was Mr. Anansi and Tumble-bug. Deh was a young lady, was de king daughter. Her fader said who come wid a jar of money will get dat young lady to marry. Tumble-bug get a jar of money. Anansi get a jar an' couldn't get no money to put in it, get some cow dung an' some horse dung fill up de jar.

And after dem was going up to de young lady, dem ketch to a shop. And de two jar favor one anodder. An' Anansi said, "Brar Tumble-bug, let we go in de shop go get a drink." An' Anansi said, "Mus' buy a bread come," an' as he come out, him tak up Tumble-bug jar and let' fe him jar. An' Tumble-bug tak up Anansi jar.
And when dem go up to de young lady in de king yard, Anansi said, "Massa, mus' bring a clean sheet go t'row out money out of jar!" An' he t'row out money—wa-a-a-a! An' as Tumble-bug t'row, him t'row out horse-dung an' cow-dung.

Anansi said, "Tak it up, tak it up, tak it up, you nasty fellow, carry out de missis yard!" Dat is why you see Tumble-bug roll in filth to-day to-day.I

Why John Crow Has a Bald Head
by Margaret Brown, St. Anne's Bay

Anansi always has a grudge wid John-crow; he say whenever he make his nest, de Crow fly on it an' catch it up an' he never can make his nest, so he have a hatred for Crow. He say he was going to married and he was going to invite no one but Crow.

An' he have a big dinner an' no one was at de table but Crow. So after de eat an' drink done, he said he was going to have a baptism but he don't baptize wid not'ing but boiling water. So after de water's boiling, he took it off an' order Crow to sit round de copper an' so he dip ev'ry one head into de water, an' dat why Crow have bald-head to-day.

The Dance
by Henry Spence, Bog, Westmoreland

Anansi and John Crow had a ball one night, so dey fin' dinner de night fe all de dancer. John Crow a great 'tepper, can 'tep better'n Anansi. So as Anansi fin' John Crow can dance neater dan him, he get bex. So after de dinner de pop was hot, so he said to John Crow him mus' dance up to de pop. So jus' to get rid of John Crow de night, he got a ladle an' dash on John Crow wid de hot pop right up on de head, an' all John Crow head 'trip off. All de John Crow in dis worl' never have ne feder upon i' head heah; Anansi bu'n 'em off wid hot pop.

Why Dog Is Always Looking
by Moses Hendricks, Mandeville

Anansi and Dog were friends. They wanted to go into cultivation, so both of them went out in search of good lands to rent. They came across a nice bit of land. Anansi fell in love with the spot; Dog fell in love with the spot too. Anansi said to Dog he remembered when he was a little boy his father planted yams on that very spot of land,—"An' the yams did bear." Dog said, "How they bear big?" Anansi said, "Brar Dog, they bear big, they bear big like me leg!" (Anansi's leg is jus' like a thread!) Brar Dog say, "Before I work an' plant yam, an' the yam not bigger than you. leg, I sooner walk round an' look!" That's the reason why, when you're eating, a dog 'sure to be looking at you.

Why Rocks at the River Are Covered with Moss
by Sarah Vassel, Bog, Westmoreland

Anansi was gwine out one day an' he stop a ribber-side a-eatin'. A rock-stone beg him, an' wouldn't gi' him none. After eat done, wan' to get up; rock-stone hol' him an' he couldn't get up. An' began to bawl.

A man was coming pas' same time an' ask him, "Bredder Anansi, who been a cry heah?" Anansi said, "Don' know!" An' de man go inside de bush, go hide. Anansi holla, an' he come out an' he catch him by his two han' an' draw him right tip.

Half a him 'kin lef' on de stone. Moss a grow upon rock-stone a ribber-side, Anansi skin a grow deah.

Why Ground Dove Complains
by Simeon Falconer, Santa Cruz Mountains

Tiger planting corn, and birds and everyt'ing destroying de corn, so him get Dove to help him fe watch who is destroying de corn. So after dey sit up de whole night fo' to watch de corn, next day Tiger him go sleep. Bredder Dove go back in de day now and destroy de corn. So de nex' day, Tiger went in de day and dodge in de ground. Bredder Dove have a gang, an' Tiger were slap him on de ears and he sing out, "Me ears! me ears! me ears!" An' from dat day to dis de dove singing, "Me ears!"

Why Hog Is Always Grunting
by Norman Hilton, Harmony Hall

Brar Hog and Brar Dog live close by river-side, so Brar Dog said to Brar Hog, "Come! we get a bathe!" Brar Hog said yes, so Brar Hog took off his mout' and Brar Dog an' Brar Hog jump in the water.

Brar Dog said to Brar Hog, "Come! let us see who can dive longer than the other." So two of them dive underneath the water. Brar Dog come up, jump out of the water, take Brar Hog mout' and went away with it.

When Brar Hog come out of the water, searching for his mout' and couldn't fin' it, an' said, "Humph! Brar Dog tak a me mout'!" That's why Brar Hog always grunting.

Why Toad Crokes
by Richard Morgan, Sonia Cruz Mountains

One man got a darter. He said, "Got one cotton tree; de man cut dat cotton tree, he marry to me darter." Every man go cut, soon dey cut de chip fasten back; so dem couldn't get de girl to marry. Toad said him go fall him. Toad full in pocket a hashes an' every chop him chop him fling de hashes upon de tree when de chip fly, and 'ey kyan't fasten. So Toad do an' do till he fell de cotton tree.

De master hab a long barbecue an' tell him say, "Now you mus' go down dere and 'trip yo'self an' I wi' pour on de water to let you skin." All dis time one big pot hot water on de fire boil up, so dem turn over de pot o' hot water an' say, "Brar Toad, water come! tak you rubbin' clot'." An' Toad jump in wild pine; up to dis day, ev'ry night you hear him cry out, "Kwoka soaka!"

Why Woodpecker Bores Wood
by Samuel Wright,
Maroon Town, Cock-pit Country

There was a bird name of Woodpecker promise his mother to bury him into a stone, an' go all about an' tell all his frien' dat him gwine to bury him mother into a stone.

An' de mother was poorly unto death an' he went to go an' bore a stone, an' he turn back an' said, "Mother, I try the stone but I can't bore it. I'll bury you into a wood."

An' he bore de wood. An' after de death of his mother, he buried him into a wood. That is the reason the woodpecker bore the wood.

Why Crab Is Afraid After Dark
by Richard Morgan, Santa Cruz Mountains

Crab go to God to gi' him head. God tell him he mus' go back, "Tomorrow come, I will give you head."

After Crab gwine home, he rej'ice into him, he singin',
"T'ank God, tomorrow God a'mighty gi' me head!
"T'ank God, tomorrow God a'mighty gi' me head!"

He dance until he muddy de water. Nex' day he went to God a'mighty fe get head. God tell him say, "Stop! after you don' get head yet you go an' muddy water; den if you get head you will do worse. So you mus' carry your head upon your shoulder all de days of you life."

So when Crab returning home, when him ketch Orange Bay an' stan' der call Daniel name, said him wouldn't trust a shadder after dark, for him don't know when dey pick him up t'row him into his basket.

Why Mice Are No Bigger
by Richard Morgan, Santa Cruz Mountains

Deh is, a man de name of Robin Mice-rat gwine to his uncle house. Him an' de uncle stay dere in dark de whole time. When him gwine away, he tell de uncle good-by an' tak a stick an' he lick 'e uncle. At dis time he went to our Saviour an' said he want to turn big man, so de Savior tell him say if he wan' to turn big man he mus' go an' kill his oldest uncle. So, as he never died, he went back de nex' night. So him an' his uncle talking an' his uncle said to him, "Dat fellow Robin come here las' night; when him gwine away, tak a stick an' lick me in de head. But, me pickney, if a heah (pointing to the temple) him ketch me, de fellow would a got me." So as de uncle show him de place, as him get up, meet his uncle at de said place, kill him 'tiff dead.

Nex' day he went to his Savior fe let him turn big man. De Savior said to him, "You little bit of man go kill you' oldest uncle, den if me let you turn bigger you will do worse!" So from dat day das de reason let you see mice don't bigger to dis day.

Rat's Wedding
by Thomas Williams,
Harmony Hall, Cock-pit Country

Rat got married, an' dere was rice and peas provide for de helping of food fe de dinner. It was so richly cook an' so much dat it get burn. So Rat remember dat de rice burn in de pot, an' Rat like 'crapin', an' while he was goin' home wid his wife in de way, when he get part way he said to her, "I forget somet'ing very valuable in de wedding house, have to go back fe it!"

She said yes, an' put out de buggy on de water-table an' run back to de wedding house, never went in where everybody in de house merrying himself, went to de kitchen. So de pot wid de bu'n rice was lean up by de side of de wall. So de force he go to de pot wid trouble de pot, an' de pot, 'stead of rolling away, tu'n over cover him underneat'. An' when he fin' dat he couldn't come out, he said, "Chut! what about dat? I wouldn't give a biscuit fe a man who kyan't lose his night rest!" and he begin to 'crape bu'nt part kur-ur-rup krup krup krup.

His wife calling now, "Mr. Rat! Mr. Rat!"—"Me head fasten in pot o!" Tu'n back 'crape 'crape. So de cook hear de noise and went out in de kitchen, find it was Rat underneat' de pot an' call out fe help. An' come out lift up de pot an' kill him. Dat's why so many widows in de world, because dere husband died and left 'em.

(A wooden foot-path is laid above the level of high water at the side of a road likely to be flooded in high water. This is called a 'water table'.)

Cockroach's Breakfast
by Richard Morgan, Santa Cruz Mountains

One day Cockroach said lo Cock, "Brar Cock, get little breakfas' so I will come an' have breakfas' wid you." Cock said yes. Cockroach come, Cockroach eat.

When he done 'e said, "Brat Cock, when you know time my breakfas' ready, come." Cock said, "How mus' I know?" Cockroach said, "I wi' gi' you a sign. When you hear I mak noise, don' come; but when you hear I stay still in de yard, you mus' come."

When Cock go, he didn't fin' Cockroach. Cock return back to his yard. Secon' day, Cockroach come an' say, "O Brat Cock! from I lef' you heah, pain all over my skin so I go an' lie down, I couldn't look a t'ing; but t'-day you can come."

Cock do de same, go to de yard, didn't fin' him, return back. When he ketch half way, he hear in Cockroach house,

"Ring a ting ting,
Me know nigger fe nigger!"

Cock tak time, tip on him toe. An' go long to one gourd, he hear Cockroach in a de gourd. An' Cock tak him bill, lick him at de gourd.

Cockroach run out. Cock pick him up an' swaller him. So from dat day, not a cockroach walk a fowl yard any more.

The Drum
by Mrs. Matilda Hall, Harmony Hall

Once there is Dog, Monkey, Tiger, Puss and Cockroach. So Christmas coming and hear them playing all about music and them has none. An' said, "We have to make up to make a drum now, then how will we manage?" So they says, "The only way, we have to cut a little little of our skin to make a drum." The Roach said, "I have none", so them drive him out of the company and he got into a banana tree to live; then he turned round to them and said, "I first will play that drum!"—"How will you get it to play?" them ask him, an' said, "I first will play it!"

Well, them fit up the drum now with the skin, hang it up to get cure. So Christmas Eve fall now. Then going to the market to buy up all them things, catch about three quarter of a mile they heard the drum playing, said, "Biddy bwoy! who playing our drum?"

So it is Roach took down the drum, put it between his feet and began to play;
"Kelly money better kelly better,
Kelly money better kelly better,
Tira coota na tira ding ding,
Tira coota na tira ding ding!"

is the Roach singing. The Puss come see him and kill him, and Puss eat Roach until this day.

Hunter, Guinea Hen and Fish
by Thomas Williams,
Harmony Hall, Cock-pit Country

Hunter always hunting an' he meet up a splendid piece of land, rich land, and he t'ink to cultivate it an' he begin same day cut bush. Piece of land is Guinea-hen feeding-ground. Guinea-hen come out at night,—Guinea-hen don' walk in de day. "Massa is good, know dis is my feedin' ground an' begin to clean it so I can get my pullin' clear! Let me help myself." Make a little chopping himself too.

Ol' man coming in de morning. "Hi! t'ankful! I commence work yesterday, do somet'ing good an' massa help me!" Start to do a little himself 'side what he do first day. T'ird day come, he burn what he cut, an' Guinea-hen burn dere too. Ol' man come in morning say, "Hi! t'ankful! massa burn de balance!" Begun to clean up. Guinea-hen come de night, give t'anks an' clean up de balance of what de ol' man lef'.

Nex' day, ol' man t'ankful, begun to plant peas an' corn. Guinea-hen come in night, say, "Massa is good! I don' need to plant any", begin to eat dat which de ol' man plant. Ol' man come in de morning see de damage, say, "Hi! what insec' do dis?" Plant some more.

Go on so until de peas begin to ripe—about eight weeks. Ol' man say, "Goin' to gadder it in to-morrow." Guinea-hen hear what ol' men say, went to de sea an' call de fish wid his trombone an' tell de fish what he want: "I plant a bit of corn and peas, an' gettin' ripe an' ol' man coming to-morrow an' I wan' to go to-night gadder it in before he come to-morrow."

Fish accept an' say, "Well, yes, I'll go, but, Friend Guinea-hen, I kyan' walk an' I kyan' fly, my wing is not strong enough. So, as you have foot an' wing, you give me one of dem, I'll go." Guinea-hen says, "Yes, I'll lend you my wing but I kyan' tak me legs off to give you. See de straight road? You can fly an' drop, an' I'll run on quick on my feet." So Fish fly an' drop, an' Guinea-hen run on till came to de groun'. "Here is my own field; gadder an' eat as much as you like."

When day commence to light, de time man is to come, Guinea-hen commence to eat an' look out. Fish say, "What you lookin' so fo', Friend Guinea-hen?" Guinea-hen see ol' man coming, say, "It's a butterfly I see jumpin' about. Lend me yo' wings, I go ketch it fe you." An' he sail away quietly out of groun'. Ol' man come, see damage an' begin to grumble an' pick what he can till he get whe' de Fish is, say, "Lawd I see him whe' he mak him bed!" an' when he hawl up a big root an' see Fish a-flutt'ring an' a-trembling, he say, "O Fish! is it you do dis damage all dis time?"

Fish says, "No, not I! Don' kill me an' I sing you some song." Ol' man like music, put him in a tub o' water to sing an dance.

Fish says, "Tak me to de neares' sea-side you has!" Ol' man tak up de tub, put it on his head goin' to de sea-side. Fish begin,
"She man yerry me bra, hay!
She man yerry me bra!
Guinea, guinea, quot amba tory."

Ol' man dance, Fish sing, until big wave coming an' Fish aim for it an' go long wid it. Ol' man stay dancing, don' know dat Fish is gone. Look in tub, Fish gone. Run home fe hook an' line an' t'row it into de sea to catch Fish. An' dat is why we always have to catch fish at sea.

The Tar Baby
by Rennie Macfarlane, Mandeville

When Brer Fox tried to catch Brer Rabbit, he could not catch him. He stick up a tar-pole in his common, an' when Brer Rabbit come an' see it', say, "Come out of Brer Fox place or I kick you!" An' the tar-pole wouldn't come out, An' kick him an' his foot fasten. "Let go foot, else I kick you with the other one!" An' he won't let it go, an' kick it with the other one an' the other foot fasten. An' he box him an' his han' fasten. An' say, "Let go me, else I box you!" an' he box him with the other han' an' his han' fasten. An' he said, "Let it go, else I buck you!" An' he buck him an' head fasten. An' said, "Let me go, else I bite you!" an' when he bite him, mouth fasten an' he couldn't move or talk.

An' Brer Fox said, "Think I couldn't catch you!" An' Brer Fox said, "Out of burn you an' drown you an' hang you an' dash you over de bramble, which one you rather?" He said, "Do anything you like but don' dash me over dat bramble!" An' Brer Fox take him an' dash him over the bramble, an' he said, "Oh, what a fool!"

Saying Grace
by Rennie Macfarlane, Mandeville

Brer Fox catch Brer Rabbit again. So he gwine kill him, an' Brer Rabbit said, "Do, Brer Fox, as you gwine kill me, have prayers. An' he said, "Clasp you hands an' say what I say: 'O God, bless an' blind us!'" but Brer Fox thought he say "Bless an' help us," an' he say it. An' Rabbit run away an' they never see him.

Pretending Dead
by Rennie Macfarlane, Mandeville

When Brer Fox want to get Brer Rabbit again, he an' Bear make up to catch him. Brer Bear go to Brer Rabbit yard an' tell him that Brer Fox dead an' he mus' help him bury him, for he an' Brer Fox friends.

When he go to Brer Fox yard, be see Brer Fox lying down. Brer Rabbit put on his bonpon hat an' coatie an' spectacle an' sit up in a rocking-chair an' say, "I never see it so! What a style! what a funniness! I think that when folks fall down die, they always cock up their foot in the air an' make 'pooh!'"

An' Brer Fox cock up his foot in the air an' say, "Pooh!" an' Brer Rabbit go away an' say, "A man like you never dead yet!"

Horse and Turtle
by Alfred Williams,
Maroon Town, Cock-pit Country

Horse bet Turtle say a get to Kingston before him. Turtle bet him say him will get to Kingston before him, Brar Horse. An' Turtle tak up one of him pickney an' drop dem ev'ry mile-post, an' drop de last one in at Kingston at de wharf-house, tell 'im 'em going for a sack of salt. An' de night when dem start, as Brar Horse catch to de firs' mile-post an' sing out in a harsh note,

I-ya-a ya-o sa, nom-be, ya-o ya ya-o sa-a, nom-be,
a nom-be, sa-ka be-ne sa-bi-na, nom-be, ya ya-o sa, a, nom-be.

Turtle answer quite yonder, soft an' sweet,

I-ya-a ya-o sa-a, nom-be, ya-o sa ya-o sa-a, nom-be,
se sa-ka be-ne sa-bi-na, nom-be, ya ya-o sa-a, nom-be.

Horse say, "Well! Brar Turtle gone!" Gallop, draw rein an' 'pur

As he get to de nex' mile-post, hear,

"I-ya-a ya-o sa, nom-be, ya-o ya."
Gallop an' gallop till he get to de nex' mile-post.

Turtle sing,

"I-ya-a ya-o sa, nom-be, ya-o ya."

Trabbel on, ride on, ride on, ride on, catch to de nex' mile-post, sing out,

"I-ya-a ya-o sa, nom-be, ya-o ya."

Turtle answer de same song quite at de mile-post,—

"I-ya-a ya-o sa, nom-be, ya-o ya."

As Horse catch to dat mile-post go in to Kingston, drop down dead!

[1. A round tin cooking pot is called a "bonpon". So is a high round hat.]

Pigeon and Parrot
by Julia Gentle, Santa Cruz Mountains

Pigeon an' Parrot was co'rtin' one girl an' she say whichever one firs' come in de house de mornin' she would marry dat one. Parrot could not fly very fas'. He went an' mek bargain wid anodder Parrot. He went before an' leave de odder one to follow Pigeon behin'. He went near to de girl house an' sit down in a tree. Pigeon call, saying,

"Come on, me pretty Poll, come on, me pretty Poll,
Stay on de tree so long,
For de sun an' de moon gwine down, Stay on de tree so long."

Parrot answer Pigeon behind,
"Go on, me pretty Pigeon, go on, me pretty Pigeon,
Stay on de tree so long,
Go on, me pretty Pigeon, go on, me pretty Pigeon,
Stay on de tree so long."

Pigeon sail again. He stop, call again,
"Come on, me pretty Poll, come on, me pretty Poll,
Stay on de tree so long,
Come on, me pretty Poll, come on, me pretty Poll,
Stay on de tree so long."

Parrot answer,
"Go on, me pretty Pigeon, go on, me pretty Pigeon,

Stay on de tree so long,
Go on, me pretty Pigeon, go on, me pretty Pigeon,
Stay on de tree so long."

Pigeon sail. When Pigeon nearly catch to de house, call again in de same tune. Parrot answer before now. Pigeon say, "Stop! a lil' while Parrot was behin'; how Parrot get before?" When Pigeon went to de house, Parrot was in de house. Pigeon has to stay outside an' Parrot married to de girl.

Man Is Stronger
by Simeon Falconer, Santa Cruz Mountains

The Lion and the Tiger were very good friends. Tiger says, "No one beat us in strength!" Lion said, "No, my friend, somebody that's stronger than we. Tiger said no, no, he cannot believe that. Lion said there was a little something called "Man" that was stronger. So Tiger says he will have to find that something called 'Man."

And he go hunting the Man and he buck up Mr. Ram-goat and he ask him if him name "Man". Goat says yes. And he asked him if the two things he had up here (horns) called "gun". And he asked him if that long scat he have on belly, called "ram-rod." And he asked him if that bag he had, called "shot-bag." And Goat said yes. And Tiger walk up and lick him flat on the ground. Goat holla, "Wi-i! wi-i-i!" And Tiger went back to Lion and say he find something called "Man" and single lick he lick him, fa' dead. Lion say, "No, me friend! dat no 'Man', for Man have two feet an' dat you tell me have four legs." Tiger say will have to go back again find Man, for he bound to have that something called "Man".

And he went out again seeking after "Man", and a Hunter was out. And he saw the Hunter and he said, "Now this yeah mus' Man!" And so him gwine up to de man, de Hunter aiming for him with the gun, and ask if him name "Man". And the Hunter drive at him with the gun. And he run back to Lion and could only say, "I find 'Man' an' him single answer him answer me, blood fly all t'ru me body!" and him dead. Lion says, "I tell you; you no believe me; but you believe me now!""

Anansi and Rabbit

Brar Nansi and Brar Rabbit went for a walk one day. Brar Rabbit ask Brar Anansi to show him 'daytime trouble'.

An' while dey go on, Brar Anansi saw Tiger den wid a lot of young Tiger in it. Brar Anansi took out one an' kill it an' give Rabbit a basket wid a piece of de Tiger's meat to carry for de Tiger's fader, an' took Rabbit along wid him to Tiger's house an' tol' Brar Rabbit to han' Tiger de basket.

Anansi run, an' Tiger catch at Rabbit to kill him, but he get away. Brar Anansi run up a tree an' say, "Run, Brar Rabbit, run! run fe stone-hole!" Took a razor an' give it to Rabbit.

An' Tiger got up a lot of men to get Rabbit out de hole an' Tiger sent for Reindeer to dig him out, as he had a long neck to put down his head an' dig him out; but Anansi tol' Rabbit when Reindeer put down his head in de hole, he mus' tak de razor an' cut it off.

A lot of people gadder to see Reindeer tak Rabbit out of de hole, but instead, Reindeer head was taken off an' he drop an' was dead an' de whole crowd run away wid fright.

After Rabbit come out, Brar Nansi say to him,

"Brar Rabbit, so 'daytime trouble' stay. So, as long as you live, never ask anybody to show it to you again!

Big Bwoy Stories

One of the ladies in the church Sister Lovena Burrowes was always telling me Big Boy stories and that is how I came to here of them. They always had a moral side to them in our conversations. I wrote down the stories that she would tell me.

I researched and learned that Big Bwoy is a humorous lead character of the Jamaican big bwoy (boy) stories. Big Bwoy stories go back to the 1920's in Jamaica. Big Bwoy (boy) is a quintessential, large clueless but endearing character whose adventures keep children in stitches. His wit allows him to triumph by the back door, subverting authority of adults, teachers, school inspectors and what they try to teach him.

Big Bowy and Gee Gee

One morning Big Bwoy did late fi school so 'im ride 'im father donkey, 'Gee Gee', go a school. Him did in such a hurry dat him nevah tie di donkey propaly. Well, guess wha happen? In di midst a spelling class, Gee Gee get loose. Big Bwoy frighten so till wen him look out a di window an see di donkey a gallop wey. Meanwhile, di teacher ask de class, 'Children, how do you spell egg?' Big Bwoy nah listen di teacher, him only waan di donkey fi stop, so him shout out, 'EE GEE GEE!' (A common way to quiet horses and donkeys is to say, 'Ee Boy, Ee')

Big Bwoy, Math Class and Zero

Big Bwoy inna math class an di teacher show the class about zero's. Big Bwoy come from class and tell his mudder that he learned about zeros and she say that is nuttin. Then she sends Big Bwoy go bank and get her $20.00. Big Bwoy add two more zero's and bring back $200.00 and when she see dat she scream, say you draw out all my money and Big Bwoy say "you say zeros are nuttin".

Big Bwoy, Math Class and Biscuits

One Day Big Bwoy was sitting in de back of class when teacher ask

"Class if I have 7 biscuits and I add 5 more to it how many do I have?" A next yute next to Big Bwoy whisper low "12?"

Big Bwoy hear dis and shout out "12 teacher, 12!!!"

Teacher startled and shocked said, "Big Bwoy, I cyan believe it! After all dees years you finally answer a question correct. For dat I am going to give you 12 biscuits."

Big Bwoy say, "Chuh if me did know, me wudda se hundred!"

Big Bwoy and Composition Class

Big Bwoy inna composition class an di teacher ask 'im fi mek a sentence wid 'defence, defeat and detail'. Guess wha Big Bwoy say? 'De dawg jump over de fence an de feet go before de tail'.

Big Bwoy and the Car Accident

Big Buoy wen a walk pon de road and car lick im dong, him when a bleed and him did knock out. Somebady say: "Get di buoy som suga and wata nuh". Di Big Buoy git up and say "Get mi som bun and cheese too".

Big Bwoy and the Ark

Big bwoy being in class and the teacher asked… "Who built the ark?" Other student: "Big Boy, you know?" Big Bwoy: "Know wha??"Teacher: "That is right, Big Bwoy, Noah built the ark"

Big Bwoy and Spelling Class

Big Bwoy in class an him teacher ask him fi spell the word INK. Big Bwoy looked puzzled cause him couldn't spell the word. Same time him friend lean over an she say, "Big Bwoy if yuh don't spell the word Miss gwane beat yuh." Big Bwoy say 'I aint care'. Miss say what was that you said big bwoy. Him repeat 'I aint care', then Miss say "good Big Bwoy, I-N-K.

Big Bwoy and Da Plane

One day Big Bwoy go a school an di teacher say everybaddy fi draw sup n. So when di teacha luk pan everybaddy drawing di teacha seh good good. Den when it reach to Big Boy him come up an di teacha dey dey a luuk pan. Di paypa an she but Big Bwoy mi no see nutn me ongle see waan likkle dat. So hair Big Boy him now yes teacha es a plane but it dey far out u caaan seet.

Big Bwoy and Christmas

Once upon a time, big bwoy used to walk an tief people wet clothes offa line. One day, sista Pooncie wash two pillah case an a brown banlon, an pin dem pon de line while she a clean fe Chrustmus. When she go back roun a back, de line empty!
De dawg him outta street a mek war. Suh trap set fe de tief.

Well, de trap day in question, one piece a washing puddung. Mary bring ova fe har bed spread weh did come eena barrel fram Henglan. An Icy bring har flowaz curtain. All ooman go eenside an shet de door. Wid yeye ball a peep through door an windah creases.

Den now, bout six man wid six machete spread out a de four kanah a de yard. Dis in case dis tief decide fe try get weh. Well, dem wait an wait an wait, notta soun. Till de gate creak huppen, an in walks Big Bwoy.

Big Bwoy weh shoob foot under Pooncie dining table an eat har fry egg an bread. Drink har milo. A pinchy coby pon him two toe pint inna Pooncie backyard wid crocus bag fe come tief off har clothes offa de line. Suh, as him raise him han to de fuss clothes pin, Pooncie bawl out "Teeeef!!"

An' as faas as lightning, one heap sword fight machete come dung outta nowehere. Pitch him dung pon him back like dead cockroach.

Dem nayly kill him wid beaten! Pooncie a fling water pon him fe mek certain him still libbing.

Well, Christmus Eve come, an widout money but determine nuffi go back go tief people wet clothes offa line an selly, Big Bwoy go tun bell ringer outta store doorway fe Salvation Army. Hoping seh if him ring de bell, an put on a little one-man show, people woulda drap money inna de bucket. But dem woulda also drap some inna fe him butter pan. Suh hear him:

"Ear ye, ear ye. Jesus a go come back. Woe to de man weh miss de signs a de laas days! Woe to de man weh refuse fi gi to de work a de Almighty kingdom. Brimstone an fire in de laas days!"

Said time, de bungle a people weh draw near fe hear, begin drap money inna de bucket an inna de butter pan. Hoping seh Massa God a notice. Fe spare dem fram de brimstone.

Suh Big Bwoy gone on: "Yea, in de last days, Him a go call Peter de rock. But de church a go rupcha like smady appendix."

All on a sudden Big Bwoy demeanour start change. Suh smady weh realise what a galang, raise a sankey: "Abide with me. Faas faaaall da heveling tiiiide!!"
An suh dem a drag de sankey, a suh dem a wipe yeye water. An suh de Spirit a tek ova, a suh Big Bwoy overcome wid boldness:

"An Matthew seh, this gospel of the Kingdom will be preached in all the world as a witness to all the nations, and then the end will come. And Daniel chapter 12 verse 2 seh many of those who sleep in the dust of the earth shall awake, some to everlasting life, some to shame and everlasting contempt." Alleluia, Alleluia!

An as Big Bwoy surrender to Jesus Christ pon da piazza dat Christmus eve mawning, him experience de truc mcaning a Christmas. That God sen Him Son fe save de laas.

Suh, empty pocket, him carry de butter pan a money an de red bucket an han it ova to de head office.

But God had a plan. Dem hire him fe wash an sort out clothes fe homeless people. Missis, when yu know de Christ, all things work fe good eeh? Merry Christmas and a happy New Year!

Jamaica Child
by Errol O'Connor

Big Bwoy & Likkle Bwoy

Once upon a time dere was two bradders one name Big Bwoy and de ada Name Likkle Bwoy. Big Bwoy was de oldest, but 'im was a bit stupid in de 'ead Likkle Bwoy was de cleva one, he always tricking Big Bwoy. So one day, Likkle Bwoy tell Big Bwoy dat if Big Bwoy get in a crocus bag and let 'im tie up de top den 'im could sell it like banana and den dem could mek a lata money. Big Bwoy t'ink fa a while, but all 'im was t'inking of was de big bulla cake 'im could buy in de shop. After Big Bwoy drop dreaming 'bout de cake dem, 'im agree.

Big Bwoy got in de crocus bag and Likkle Bwoy tie it up quick, quick wid a piece of wiss, den 'im bore small small 'ole in de bag, so dat Big Bwoy could breathe. Likkle Bwoy, neva plan fe give Big Bwoy any a de money, 'im did want it all fa 'imself. He carry Big Bwoy to de roadside and every baddy pass, Likkle Bwoy tell dem dat 'im have some banana in a de crocus bag, and if dem want fe buy it.

Likkle Bwoy was dere a lang time, but nobaddy never want no banana. Likkle Bwoy was jus' a go let Big Bwoy out de crocus bag, when a man ask 'im wat 'im a sell. Likkle Bwoy tell 'im, 'im a sell banana, so de man buy de banana dem. De man was a big ad strong, im tek up the crocus wid Big Bwoy in it and trow it pan 'im shoulders, like it was really a likkle banana in de bag. Likke Bwoy tek off at top speed when 'im get 'im money. De man neva look in a de bag, but jus' pick it up and walk away. Likkic bwoy t'ink dat when de man fine Big Bwoy in he bag, 'im woulda beat 'im and tek 'im to de police, to put in jail. But de man neva do that, when 'im fine out, cause when 'im a walk down de road he 'ear sunting a breathe 'ard in de bag, and 'im know dat banana no breathe.

De man put down de bag, an fine Big Bwoy in it, wid crocus bag fluff ina 'im hair and pan 'im face. De man ask Big Bwoy wey 'im a do in de bag, an' Big Bwoy tell 'im dat 'im bradder trick 'im. Big Bwoy start fe like sumbaddy a kill 'im but de man feel sarry fe Big Bwoy and give 'im lata money, cause 'im was kind and know dat Big Bwoy was a bit fu-fool. Big Bwoy pic' up de crocus bag an' tek aff fa de shop fe buy 'im bulla cake. Den 'im go an' show Likkle Bwoy all de money 'im did 'ave. When Likkle Bwoy see all de cake dat Big Bwoy gat 'im vex, 'cause Big Bwoy mek more money dan 'im. Next day Likkle Bwoy tell Big Bwoy fe tie up de crocus bag wid 'im in it. Big Bwoy neva t'ink two time dis time, 'im tie up de Likkle Bwoy in de crocus bag and tek 'm down to de roadside an stan' dere. Big Bwoy neva stan' dere lang before de same man dat give Big Bwoy de money de day before come an buy de bag wid Likkle Bwoy. When Likkle Bwoy feel de bag liff up in de air 'im start fe t'ink 'ow de man a go give 'im a lat a money, den 'im a go run wey an nobaddy a go ketch 'im. Big Bwoy never stop fe share de money wid Likkle Bwoy, 'im tek aff fe buy 'im bulla cake. Likkle Bwoy feel when de man put down de crocus bag, an' get ready fe come out. Likkle Bwoy start fe fret, when de man tek so lang fe open de bag. Den 'im greediness lef 'im, 'im decide fe run wey, when de man open de bag. But de man never open de bag, 'im go an cut a big guava whip an give Likkle Bwoy some rawted licks. Dats time Big Bwoy a sit down a 'eat 'im cake dem. After a while de man open de bag. Likkle Bwoy tek off faster dan lightning, nat even de wind coulda ketch 'im. 'Im was black and blue all over. From den on, Likkle Bwoy neva trick Big Bwoy again.

Proverbs

The Bibical Book of Proverbs

The Book of Proverbs is God's wisdom is for living in God's world.

In my book, "Book of Wisdom Proverbs for a Hungry Soul" the first examples of proverbs we find are written by Kings Solomon. King Solomon was known for his wisdom, his wealth and his writings. In the Book of Proverbs, Solomon reveals the mind of God in matters high and lofty and in common, ordinary, everyday situations, too. It appears that no topic escaped King Solomon's attention.

Matters pertaining to personal conduct, sexual relations, business, wealth, charity, ambition, discipline, debt, child-rearing, character, alcohol, politics, revenge, and godliness are among the many topics covered in this rich collection of wise sayings.

Proverbs is the greatest "how-to" book ever written and those who have the good sense to take Solomon's lessons to heart will quickly discover godliness, prosperity, and contentment are theirs for the asking.

Some Verses from Proverbs in the New Internatioanl Version

Proverbs 1: 5 "Let the wise listen and add to their learning, and let the discerning get guidance."

Proverbs 1: 7 "The fear of the LORD is the beginning of knowledge, but fools despise wisdom and discipline."

Proverbs 4: 5 "Get wisdom, get understanding; do not forget my words or swerve from them."

Proverbs 8: 13-14 "To fear the LORD is to hate evil; I hate pride and arrogance, evil behavior and perverse speech. Counsel and sound judgment are mine; I have understanding and power."

Proverbs 10: 8 "The wise in heart accept commands, but a chattering fool comes to ruin."

Proverbs 15: 14 "The discerning heart seeks knowledge, but the mouth of a fool feeds on folly.

Proverbs 27: 3 "for he is the kind of man who is always thinking about the cost. Eat and drink," he says to you, but his heart is not with you.

Proverbs 30: 32 "If you have played the fool and exalted yourself, or if you have planned evil, clap your hand over your mouth!

The recurring promise of the Book of Proverbs is that those who choose wisdom and follow God will be blessed in numerous ways:

With Long Life

For through me your days will be many, and years will be added to your life. (Proverbs 9: 11)

Prosperity

Thus you will walk in the ways of good men and keep to the paths of the righteous. 21 For the upright will live in the land, and the blameless will remain in it; but the wicked will be cut off from the land, and the unfaithful will be torn from it. (Proverbs 2: 20-22)

Joy

Blessed is the man who finds wisdom, the man who gains understanding, 14 for she is more profitable than silver and yields better returns than gold. She is more precious than rubies; nothing you desire can compare with her. Long life is in her right hand; in her left hand are riches and honor. Her ways are pleasant ways, and all her paths are peace. She is a tree of life to those who embrace her; those who lay hold of her will be blessed. (Proverbs 3: 13-18)

The Goodness of God

No harm befalls the righteous, but the wicked have their fill of trouble. (Proverbs 12: 21)

Rejection of God

Those who reject Him, on the other hand, suffer shame and death. The wise inherit honor, but fools he holds up to shame The lips of the righteous nourish many, but fools die for lack of judgment. To reject God is to choose folly over wisdom and is to separate ourselves from God, His Word, His wisdom and His blessings. (Proverbs3: 35; Proverbs10: 21).

Jamaican Proverbs in Patios Language

According to Dr. Rebecca Tortello, Jamaican "Proverbs can be defined as short excerpts from stories about life's lessons." In Jamaica life's lessons are hard and stem from the root of slavery unwillingly inflicted upon them.

Jamaicans speak a unique version of English like no one else in the world. Below is a sampling of what some "English experts" have labeled "Patois" but what Jamaicans call "Real English".

These Proverbs are translated into Patois with the Meanings

Proverb: "When ashes cold dawg sleep in deh."
Translation: When ashes get cold then dogs will sleep in it.
Meaning: When the glory of importance fades, people take advantage of the situation.

Proverb: "Sorry fi mawga dawg, mawga dawg tun roun' bite yuh."
Translation: Show a starving dog pity and he will bite you anyway
Meaning: Empathize with a person in a problematic situation, and sometimes when things clear up later the person hurts you by his ingratitude.

Proverb: "Puss and dawg no ad de same luck."
Translation: Cats and Dogs will not have similar luck
Meaning: To each person come different opportunities.

Proverb: "Many ways to 'ang a dog without putting' a rope roun' 'im neck."

Translation: Many ways to hang a dog without using a rope around his neck

Meaning: Several strategies can be used to effect the same results.

Proverb: "Scawnful dawg eat dutty pudding."
Translation: A scornful dog will end up eating dirty pudding.
Meaning: If you are proud and finiky you may have an experience which will crush your pride.

Proverb: "Kokruch noh bizniz in a fowl fight."
Translation: Cockroaches have no business in a chicken fight
Meaning: Outsiders have no business into a private problem.

Proverb: "Weh sweet nanny goat a go run 'im belly."Translation: The same thing that gives a she goat pleasure can lead to a running belly.
Meaning: The same reason that makes you happy, can be the same reason to make you sad in the future.

Proverb: "Yuh cum fi drink milk, yuh noh cum fi count cows."
Translation: You are here to drink milk not count cows
Meaning: You are here on a specific business, do not be inquisitive in what does not concern you.

Proverb: "De higher monkey clim' de mo' 'im expose."
Translation: The Higher a monkey climbs is the more exposed he becomes
Meaning: The greater the privilege, the more risky the situation and the heavier the responsibility.

Proverb: "If you get your han' in a debil mout' tek it out.
Translation: If you put your hand in the devils mouth, take it out carefully.
Meaning: Act cautiously in getting out of difficulty.

Proverb: "Finger neber say "look here," him say "look yonder."
Translation: Finger never says "look here," he says "look yonder."
Meaning: People do not usually point out their own faults.

Proverb: "Peacock hide him foot when him hear 'bout him tail."
Translation: The peacock hides his foot when he hears about his tail.
Meaning: A proud person does not like his little weaknesses exposed.

Proverb: "No wait till drum beat before you grine you axe."
Translation: Do not wait until the drum beats before you grind your axe.
Meaning: Be prepared for all eventualities.

Proverb: "You 'fraid fey eye, you neber yam head."
Translation: If you are afraid of the eye, you will hever eat the head.
Meaning: If you regard too much the good opinion of any one you will never prosper.

Proverb: "A no want a fat mek nightingale foot "tan" so."
Translation: It is noit for the want of fat that the nightingale's legs stand so.
Meaning: Do not judge by appearances.

Proverb: "Gi mi sponge fi go dry up sea."
Meaning: Giving one an impossible task to do.

Proverb: "Good fowl a go a market sensei fowl pick up themself deh follow back a dem."
Meaning: Person with class being copied by ghetto individual.

Proverb: "Fire deh a mus-mus tail him tink a cool breeze."
Meaning: Not seeing that one is heading for trouble

Proverb: "Hog picney sey momma momma how yuh mouth so long, momma sey by & by yuh wi si."
Meaning: Children questioning parents why certain things happen, mother's reply wait & you will see

Proverb: "How watah walk go a punkin belly."
Meaning: How thing happen, what will happen. (Usually used as a threat)

Proverb: "Yuh tink a one day monkey want wife?"
Meaning: Do think you won't need my help in the future? (Do not forget your friends)

Proverb: "Sarry fi mawga dawg im tun roun bite yuh."
Meaning: Help someone out of trouble he/she then is not thankfull

Proverb: "Mi come here fi drink milk, mi noh come here fi count cow."
Meaning: A reminder to conduct business in a straightforward manner.

Proverb: "The higher the monkey climbs the more him expose."
Meaning: A truly comic image if you've ever been to the zoo, and comforting to any of us whose backs have been used as a stepping-stone for someone else's success.

Proverb: "A new broom sweeps clean, but an old broom knows every corner."
Meaning: A profoundly witty statement that sums up any number of current situations, including the state of today's music.

Proverb: "Every hoe ha dem stick bush bush."
Translation: That for every size hoe there is a stick that size in the bush (or forest) for it.
Meaning: Of all that is "to each his own.

Editors Note: In Jamaica they use tools similar to a garden hoe. They use it to make a yam hill - we use it to make path. There are different sizes for different chores. So it can also mean that there is someone out there for everyone.

Proverb: "A peer rumors ah gwan."
Meaning: Its pure rumors that are going on" in other words "Its all only rumors that's being spread.

Proverb: "Did deh deh."
Meaning: I was there.

Proverb: "Im sey dat yuh was to bring ting."
Meaning: He or She said you were to bring the thing.

Proverb: "Sumody tell mi sey yuh dida talk bout mi."
Meaning: Somebody told me you were talking about me.

Proverb: "Unnu can come wid mi."
Meaning: "You all can come with me."

Proverb: "I dey 'pon haste."
Meaning: I am in a hurry.

Proverb: "Who colt de game."
Meaning: It implies that someone made a wrong move, deliberately, to change the outcome of the plan. So who colt the game? Babylon! In other words…to prevent the Dread from succeeding, Babylon colt the game, made a "wrong" move in regards to the dread.

Proverb: "Why yu fe galang so?"
Meaning: Why must you behave in such a manner?

Proverb: "Me come yah fi drink milk, me no come yah fi count cow!"
Meaning: Deliver that which you promised, don't just talk about it!)

Proverb: "Carry Go Bring Come"
Meaning: To gossip.

Proverb: "A so im tan."
Meaning: That is what he is like.

Proverb: "Tan deh!" or "yu tan deh!"
Meaning: Just you wait!

Proverb: "Tan tedy."
Meaning: Stand steady, means "hold still.

Proverb: "Bunks Mi Res."
Meaning: Catch my rest, take a nap.

Proverb: "What sweet nanny goat a go run him belly." is a cautionary Jamaican proverb.
Meaning: What tastes good to a goat will ruin his belly. In other words - the things that seem good to you now, can hurt you later.

Proverb: "Tek smadi mek poppy-show."
Meaning: Which means to make fun of someone or shame them, making them look ridiculous.

Proverb: "You too red eye."
Meaning: You're too envious.

Proverb: "Ya No See It?"
Meaning: You know?

Proverb: "Chicken merry; hawk deh (is) near."
Meaning: Every silver lining has its dark cloud. Even in the happiest times one must still be watchful.

Proverb: "Fire de a Mus Mus tail, him tink a cool breeze."
Meaning: Set a Rat's tail on fire and he's thinks there's a cool breeze. Used to describe someone or something (the system for example) that is clueless. This characterizes the delusional complacency of the upper classes.

Proverb: "I no come to hear about how horse dead an' cow fat."
Meaning: It's like telling somebody to knock off with irrelevant details.

Proverb: "Me throw me corne but me no call no fowl."
Meaning: It evokes the image of a farmer silently scattering who is saying, in effect: "Don't call yourself a chicken just because you eat my feed; I never said I was endeavoring to feed the chickens." That is, "You are who you show yourself to be, not who you might say you are."

Proverb: "Sorry for maga dog, maga dog turn round bite you."
Meaning: This metaphor extends very well to all manner and sort of do-gooding and should be considered before any hasty acts of charity!

Proverb: "Mi throw mi corn, but me no call no fowl."
Meaning: Refers to the conversational technique of throwing out a provocative statement (throw corn) in an indirect manner, thus forestalling any accusations of personal insult.

Proverb: "Sweet nanny goat have a running belly."
Meaning: It's a barnyard analogy akin to the grass is always greener, but much coarser, noting that the sweet foliage avidly sought out by the nanny goat gives it diarrhea (running belly). It's a blunt way of warning someone off temptation.

Proverb: "Everyting Crash."
Meaning: The topic is social chaos. Also, means: "come bad in de morning can't come good a evenin", And the even more pessimistic: "every day bucket go a well, one day di bucket bottom mus drop out".

Proverb: "Wanti wanti can't get it, getti getti no want it."
Meaning: The Have-nots covet what the Haves take for granted.

Proverb: "Trouble no set like rain."
Meaning: That is, unlike bad weather, we are often not warned by dark clouds on the horizon.

Proverb: "The child must "creep before him walk."
Meaning: And remember, "one one coco fill up a basket", take it easy and fill up your shopping basket one item at a time.

Proverb: "Every mikkle makes a muckle."
Meaning: Refers to thriftiness, similar to "a penny saved is a penny earned".

Proverb: "No cup no broke, no coffee no dash wey."
Meaning: Even if disaster strikes your home it's always possible that all may not be lost.

Proverb: "Heart No Leap", "See and Blind."
Meaning: These sayings are similar to "hear no evil, see no evil".

Proverb: "See an bline, hear an deaf."
Meaning: Dont talk other people business or can keep a secret.

Proverb: "Ole fia stick easy fi ketch."
Meaning: Easy to get something that you once had it before.

Proverb: "Walk better dan sidong."
Meaning: To walk is better than to sit down.
1. Used when someone goes somewhere and recieves something he or she needs or can use, that he or she might not have recieved, staying home.
2. While not in a fortunate position in life one still remains industrious.

Proverb: "Every hoe ave dem tik a bush."
Meaning: There's someone out there for everyone

Proverb: "Di fus wata hog pass him wash himself."
Meaning: Make use of the oportunities that come your way first

Proverb: "Roach nuh business inna fowl fite."
Meaning: Stay out of things that don't concern you or else.

English to Jamaican Phrases

English: "It's been a long time since I have seen you, girl."
Jamaican: "Gal yuh noh dead yet?"

English: "Lord, we have lost electricity again!"
Jamaican: "Lawd Gad, current lack aff again!"

English: "Where did you buy that awful bracelet, Cindy?"
Jamaican: "A weh yuh buy dat deh big ole ugly bangle deh, missus?"

English: "Hors d'oeuvres."
Jamaican: "Ah wah dis likkle sinting yuh a gi me?"

English: "I think something is wrong with Susan, she might have the flu."
Jamaican: "Lawd Gad, breeze tek up Suzie!"

English: "Girl, those shoes are the bomb."
Jamaican: "Gyal, yuh roach killa dem a seh one out deh."

English: "Oh my gosh, I just broke Mom's expensive plate."
Jamaican: "Lawd mi Gad, mi bruk up Mama stoosh crackry."

English: "Aren't those pants a bit short?"
Jamaican: "Yuh did a expect flood ar yuh tek yuh measurement inna wata?"

English: "Why are you squeezing the mangoes like that?"
Jamaican: "Lissen mi nuh, mi a beg yuh stap fingle-fingle up di mango dem."

English: "Sir, please don't throw my luggage like that."
Jamaican: "Aye buff teet bwoy, tap fling up-fling up mi bag dem suh man."

English: "I wish you would quit lying."
Jamaican: "Tap di lyin, yuh ole liyad."

English: "Lift the hood off the car for me, John."
Jamaican: Hey my yute, fly di bonnet!

English: "I am waiting for a taxi and it's taking so long."
Jamaican: "But wait, no Robot naw run tidey!"

English: "Get me a soda please."
Jamaican: "Beg yuh carry wan aerated wata fi mi deh."

English: "It's time for a perm."
Jamaican: "Gal yuh head waan cream, yuh noh si how it tough an tan bad!"

English: "Yuck!! This is nasty."
Jamaican: "Kiss mi neck back!! What a sinting tyase bad an incipid."

English: "Please make some room in the bus so this man can sit."
Jamaican: "Schoolas, small up unnu self man mek Daddy siddung."

English: "I have a stomach ache."
Jamaican: "Mi belly ah gripe mi."

English: "These mangoes look a bit over ripe."
Jamaican: "Missus, move fram in front ah mi wid dem fluxy mango deh."

English: "She has a bit of an overbite."
Jamaican: "Gyal fayva buckteet Ida."

English: "He has very large full eyes."
Jamaican: "Wat ah bway fayva patoo."

English: "He has no manners."
Jamaican: "I'm noh have noh broughtupsy."

English: "Perspiration odor."
Jamaican: "Him smell green."

English: "Boiled chicken."
Jamaican: "Dat deh sinting nuh staat cook yet."

English: "Oh dear."
Jamaican: "Ee-eeeee."

English: "Josh is suffering from Attention Deficit Disorder."
Jamaican: "Di pickney too hard eaize!"

English: "I need a bottle of Pepto Bismal…my stomach hurts."
Jamaican: "Lawd, mi coulda do wid a wash out yah nung…mi belly bine up."

English: "Oh my, your feet are so ashy."
Jamaican: "Yuh foot tuff laka aligata bak…yuh couldn't rub likkle coknut ile pon yuh foot?"

English: "Looking tired."
Jamaican: "Heng pan nail."

Jamaican Phrases & Their Meanings

Jamaican: "Ride & wistle"
Translation: "Be able to do more than one thing at a time,eg, talk & work."

Jamaican: "Johncrow always tink im picney pretty"
Translation: "Parent always think there children are beautiful."

Jamaican: "Me bleach hard lass night"
Translation: I partied straight through the night."

Jamaican: "Ya No See It?"
Translation: "You know?"

Jamaican: "The gal come wine up on me,"
Translation: "It would mean that the girl came and was dancing up on me."

Jamaican: "A fe me cyar."
Translation: "It's my car."

Jamaican: "Mi a go lef tiday."
Translation: "I am leaving today."

Jamaican: "Im too haad eaize."
Translation: "He/She is too stubborn."

Jamaican: "Axe har de question."
Translation: "Ask her the question."

Jamaican: "Im badda dan dem." "Nuh bodda mi."
Translation: "He is worse than they are." "Don't bother me."

Jamaican: "Bare dog dung inna dat yard."
Translation: "There are only dogs in that yard."

Jamaican: "No bodda bawl im soon cum bak."
Translation: "Don't bother crying he'll soon be back."

Jamaican: "Sell mi wan bokkle a iyl."
Translation: "Sell me a bottle of oil."

Jamaican: "Dat a mi bredda."
Translation: "That is my brother."

Jamaican: "Is who bruk de bokkle a iyl?"
Translation: "Who broke the bottle of oil?"

Jamaican: "Coodeh, yuh see de big bud eena de tree?"
Translation: "Cody, look at the big bird in the tree."

Jamaican: "Bwaay! Mi did tink de test wudda eazy."
Translation: "Boy! I though that test would have been easy.

Jamaican: "The parson sey de marriage cerfitikit soon cum inna de mail."
Translation: "The pastor said that the marriage certificate will be coming soon in the mail."

Jamaican: "Mi love chaklit cake with nuff icenin."
Translation: "I love chocolate cake with plenty of icing."

Jamaican: "Mi a go bak a wuk pan Chewsday."
Translation: "I am going back to work on Tuesday."

Jamaican: "Di chuck want tree new tyres."
Translation: "The truck will need three new tires."

Jamaican: "Cuyah, she gwan lak she nice eee?"
Translation: "Look at that, she acts like she is so nice."

Jamaican: "Chobble nuh nice." "Yuh inna big chobble."
Translation: "Trouble is not nice." "You are in big trouble."

Jamaican: "Mi cyan 'elp yuh wit dat problem."
Translation: "I cannot help you with that problem."

Jamaican: "Mi like yuh cris cyar."
Translation: "I like your new car."

Jamaican: "Yuh did see dat?" "A who dat?"
Translation: "Did you see that?" "Who is that?"

Jamaican: "Dat dawta pretty lakka money." "A fi mi dawta."
Translation: "That daughter is pretty like money." "Is my daughter."

Jamaican: "Mista Brown dawg bite mi."
Translation: "Mr. Brown's dog bit me."

Jamaican: "De bwoy dem teif di bleach outta de wata."
Translation: "The boys stole the bleach out of the water."

Jamaican: "Dem a wan no good bunch."
Translation: "They are a no good bunch."

Jamaican: "Mi did de deh pan Chewsday."
Translation: "I was there on Tuesday."

Jamaican: "Dis cyar a my own."
Translation: "This car is mine."

Jamaican: "Yuh nuh dun yet?"
Translation: "You have not finished yet?"

Jamaican: "A di dutty duppy man dweet."
Translation: "The dirty ghost did it."

Jamaican: "Ef yuh chobble 'im, me a guh bax yuh".
Translation: "If you trouble him, I am going to hit you."

Jamaican: "Ello, mi can help yuh wid someting?"
Translation: "Hello, can I help you with something?"

Jamaican: "Di wola dem a me fambly."
Translation: "All of them are my family."

Jamaican: "Yuh tuh fass and facety."
Translation: "You are too inquisitive and fresh."

Jamaican: "Yuh 'ave any flim lef inna de camera?"
Translation: "Do you have any film left in the camera?"

Jamaican: "She a mi bess bess fren."
Translation: "She is my best friend."

Jamaican: "Galang bout yuh business."
Translation: "Go along about your business."

Jamaican: "Gimme wan tall glass a wata please."
Translation: "Give me a tall glass of water please."

Jamaican: "Mass Garden a plant flowas inna de gyarden."
Translation: "Mr. Gordon is planting flowers in the garden."

Jamaican: "Who hav mi watch?"
Translation: "Who has my watch?"

Jamaican: "Mi bak a hat mi."
Translation: "My back is hurting me."

Jamaican: "Is which wan a oonu nyam mi hegg?"
Translation: "Which one of you ate my egg?"

Jamaican: "Im sey yuh fi bring di ting."
Translation: "He or She said you were to bring the thing."

Jamaican: "A wan irie likkle place."
Translation: "It's a very nice place."

Jamaican: "Mi need sum iyl fi fry de fish."
Translation: "I need some oil to fry the fish."

Jamaican: "Mi len out de money an noh mi inna wan jam."
Translation: "I lent out some money and now I am in some trouble."

Jamaican: "Jesum Peeze, a cyan bleve dat mi lose de game."
Translation: "Oh my Gosh or Wow a can't believe I lost that game."

Jamaican: "Is you cawz de accident."
Translation: "You are the one that caused the accident."

Jamaican: "Yu can cyarri dis cow pan yuh chuck?"
Translation: "Can you carry this cow on your truck?"

Jamaican: "An a jus lass nite mi di deh."
Translation: "And it was just last night I was there."

Jamaican: "A lang time mi dey inna dis yah lang line."
Translation: "Its been a long time since I have been in this long line."

Jamaican: "Lawd 'ave mercy pan Miss Percy."
Translation: "Lord have mercy on Miss Percy."

Jamaican: "Lef mi nuh."
Translation: "Leave me alone."

Jamaican: "De bwoy a de biggest liad."
Translation: "The boy is a big liar."

Jamaican: "Im get wan big lick fram de teacha."
Translation: "He got a big hit from the teacher."

Jamaican: "Beg a likkle bokkle ah milk."
Translation: "I'm asking for a little bottle of milk."

Jamaican: "Mi madda sey yuh fi lef mi."
Translation: "My mother said that you are to leave me alone."

Jamaican: "Ole still, mi si wan big maskitta pan yu foot."
Translation: "Hold still, I see a big mosquito on your foot."

Jamaican: "Im mek up im mind areddy."
Translation: "He made up his mind already."

Jamaican: "Tek de neegle an sew de peeca clawt."
Translation: "Take the needle and sew the piece of cloth."

Jamaican: "De nex time mi will buy."
Translation: "The next time I will buy."

Jamaican: "How yuh nyam summuch?"
Translation: "How do you eat so much?"

Jamaican: "Put de bag unda de seat."
Translation: "Put de bag under the seat."

Jamaican: "Mi ah de ongle one dat did stay till it dun."
Translation: "I was the only one that stayed till it was finished."

Jamaican: "Is dat ooman deh did tek mi money."
Translation: "That is the woman that took my money."

Jamaican: "Ooo goes dere?"
Translation: "Who goes there?"

Jamaican: "Yu ave any callaloo?"
Translation: "Do you have any callaloo?"

Jamaican: "Is Mista Garden pickney dem."
Translation: "It is Mr. Gordon's children."

Jamaican: "Mi wud radda yu nuh chat to mi."
Translation: "I would rather you not talk to me."

Jamaican: "See yu pan Satday."
Translation: "See you on Saturday."

Jamaican: "Put de sinting inna de bag."
Translation: "Put the something in the bag."

Jamaican: "Smaddy tell mi sey yuh did a chat bout mi."
Translation: "Somebody told me you were talking about me."

Jamaican: "Sell mi tree poun a swimps."Translation: "Sell me three pounds of shrimps."

Jamaican: "Tan deh tink sey im a guh 'elp yu."
Translation: "Stand there thinking he is going to help you."

Jamaican: "Tanks fe de glass a ice wata."
Translation: "Thanks for the glass of ice water."

Jamaican: "Tek yu time an mine it bruk."
Translation: "Take your time, you might break it."

Jamaican: "Mista Brown mi see tree bwoy inna yu mango tree."
Translation: "Mr. Brown, I saw three boys up in your mango tree."

Jamaican: "Oonu can cum wid mi."
Translation: "You all can come with me."

Jamaican: "Wattagwan wid John?"
Translation: "What's going on with John?"

Jamaican: "De wata dutty so nuh play inna it."
Translation: "The water is dirty so don't play in it."

Jamaican: "Im jook mi inna mi yeye."
Translation: "He poked me in the eye."

Jamaican: "Dry land tourist".
Translation: A Jamaican who's never been off the island but still acts like a big shot.

Jamaican: "No one cyaan test".
Translation: No one can compete with.

Jamaican: "Mi a-go lef today".
Translation: "I am leaving today"

Jamaican: "Im too hard of Aise".
Translation: "He/She is too hard of hearing"

Jamaican: "Him is badda than dem" "No badda mi".
Translation: "He is worse than they are" "Don't bother me"

Jamaican: "Is bare dog down inna that yard".
Translation: "Is only dogs in that yard"

Jamaican: "No badda bawl im soon come back".
Translation: "Don't bother crying he'll soon be back"

Jamaican: "Dat is fe mi bredda".
Translation: "That is my brother"

Jamaican: "The chuck need tree new tyres".
Translation: "The truck will need three new tires"

Jamaican: "Cuyah, she gwan like she nice eee".
Translation: "Look at that, she acts like she is so nice"

Jamaican: "Choble nuh nice" "Yuh ina big choble".
Translation: "Trouble is not nice" "You are in big trouble"

Jamaican: "Did yuh see dat?" "A who dat?"
Translation: "Did you see that" "Who is that?"

Jamaican: " Yuh no dun yet?"
Translation: "You have not finished yet?"

Jamaican: "Is the dutty duppy man dweet".
Translation: "The dirty ghost did it."

Jamaican: "Ef yuh choble him 'im me a-go hit yuh".
Translation: "If you trouble him I am going to hit you."

Jamaican: "All a dem a me fambly".
Translation: "All of them are my family."

Jamaican: "Yuh too fass and Facety".
Translation: "You are too inquisitive and fresh."

Jamaican: "Galang bout yuh business".
Translation: "Go along about you business."

Jamaican: "Mi back a hat mi".
Translation: "My back is hurting me."

Jamaican: "An a jus Lass nite mi dideh".
Translation: "And it was just last night I was there."

Jamaican: "Lef mi Nuh".
Translation: "Leave me alone."

Jamaican: "Tek de neegle an sow de piece of clawt".
Translation: "Take the needle and sow the piece of cloth."

Jamaican: "How yuh nyam so much".
Translation: "How do you eat so much?"

Jamaican: "Mi would rada you talk to mi"
Translation: "I would rather you not talk to me."

Jamaican: "Tandy tink sey im a-go help you."
Translation: "Stand there thinking he is going to help you."

Jamaican: "Tek you time an mine it bruk".
Translation: "Take your time, you might break it."

Jamaican: "Wat a liiv an bambaie."
Translation: "Leftovers are to be put aside to eat tomorrow. (What is left for by-and by).

Jamaican: "Gone a foreign"
Translation: "Gone abroad (from Jamaica).

Jamaican: "Like mi a go maas"
Translation: Chill out.

Jamaican: "Gwaan go maas"
Translation: Go cool yourself.

Jamaican: "Mi a maas a money" (or item)
Translation: It means you're going to put it away or put it one side.

Quiz Time!

Can you complete these Jamaican proverbs?

The following proverbs are written in a loose combination of standard English and patois in an attempt to reflect the two languages commonly used on the island and out of a dual respect for the fact that this will be read rather than heard and the fact that proverbs themselves are bastions of the oral tradition, having survived orally for over hundreds of years.

See if you can fill in the blanks.

1. "One, one coco ___________________ basket" (Do not expect to achieve success overnight).

2. "Every mikkle ___________________ a mukkle" (Every little bit counts).

3. "Wat doan _______________, will fatten" (Do not waste time worrying over something that does you no real harm. You may even be able to turn it around into something positive).

4. "Chicken merry, _______________ dah near" (Be vigilant as danger can be found in unexpected places).

5. "Every dawg has his day and every puss his ___________________ o'clock" and cock mouth _________________ cock. (Do not act as if you are better than others, your day will come).

6. "Wanti, wanti, cyan getti, getti, getti nuh ___________________" Also "silent rivah run deep" and "No mug no bruk, no coffee nuh dash wey" (Count your blessings and do not take what you have for granted).

7. "Sorry fi mawga dog, mawga dog wi tun round and ______________ you" (Sometimes it is those whom we help who are the least grateful).

8. "Duppy know _____________________ fi frighten" (Bullies know to pick on those least able to defend themselves).

9. "See mi a one thing, come lib with me _______________________" (To see me is one thing, to live with me, another or as in another popular saying, do not judge a book by its cover).

10. "De olda de clock, de _____________________ it wine" (The older a person is, the wiser).

11. "When coco ripe, it mus _____________________" (Actions speak louder than words).

12. "Hog say, 'de first dutty water mi ____________________, mi wash'." (Seize opportunities as they present themselves).

13. "One eye man king in ________________________ man country". (No matter how bad it seems things may be, there is always another for whom things are worse).

14. "Fool-fool pickney mek fowl _________________ away from him two time" (Never allow yourself to be fooled the same way more than once).

15. "Nuh fatten cockroach fi _________________________________ " (Do not waste time doing things for which others will be ungrateful).

16. "Saltfish sit down pon di _____________________ a wait fi bread and butter" (Lazy people wait for life's blessings to come to them).

17. "Mi old, but mi nuh ______________________________ " (Do not underestimate the value of the elderly).

18. "Disobedient pickney ___________________________ rockstone" (Disobedient children will come to a bad end).

19. "Dawg say if him have money him would buy him own ____________ " (Some people, when they wind up with money, will waste it in unnecessary things).

20. "Talk and ___________________ your tongue" (Think before you speak).

Rasta & Patois Jamaican Dictionary

A

A: prep. to as in "go a shop," from Spanish

A GO: aux w/v. going to do, as in "Me a go tell him"

A DOOR: outdoors

ACCOMPONG: n. name of Maroon warrior, Capt. Accompong, brother of Cudjo; also name of town. From the Twi name for the supreme deity

ACKEE: n. African food tree introduced about 1778. From Twi ankye or Kru akee

AKS: ask

ALIAS: adj. (urban slang) dangerous, violent

AN: than

ARMAGEDDON: the biblical final battle between the forces of good and evil. ASHAM: n. Parched, sweetened, and ground corn. From twi osiam.

B

BABYLON: the corrupt establishment, the "system," Church and State; the police, a policeman.

BAD: good, great

BAD BWAI: (bad boy) refering to a bold man; a compliment; One who has committed a crime. (rude bwai, ruddy, baddy)

BADNESS: hooligan behavior, violence for its own sake

BAFAN: clumsy; awkward

BAFANG: a child who did not learn to walk the 1st 2-7 years.

BAG-O-WIRE: a betrayer

BAGGY: underpants for a woman or child.

BALMYARD: n. place where pocpmania rites are held, healing is done, spells cast or lifted

BAKRA: white slavemaster, or member of the ruling class in colonial days. Popular etymology: "back raw" (which he bestowed with a whip.)

BALD-HEAD: a straight person; one without dreadlocks; one who works for babylon

BAMBA YAY: by and by

BAMBU: rolling paper

BAMMY: a pancake made out of cassava, after it has been grated and squeezed to remove the bitter juice.

BANDULU: bandit, criminal, one living by guile

BANDULU BIZNESS: is a racket, a swindle.

BANGARANG: hubbub, uproar, disorder, disturbance.

BANKRA: a big basket, including the type which hangs over the sides of a donkey.

BANS: from bands; a whole lot, a great deal, nuff, whole heap.

BASHMENT : party, dance, session

BAT: butterfly or moth. English bat, the flying rodent, is a rat-bat.

BATTY: bottom; backside; anus.

BATTYBWOY: a gay person

BEAST: a policeman

BEENIE: little

BEX: vex (verb), or vexed (adjective).

BHUTTU (BUHTUH): an uncouth, out of fashion, uncultured person, Use: Wey yu a go inna dem deh cloze? Yu fayva buttu

BIG BOUT YAH : Large and in charge. Superlative indicating status (power, fame, money, talent, etc) within some social group

BISSY: cola nut.

BLACKHEART MAN: a rascal, a hooligan

BLY: chance, "must get a bly", "must get a chance".

BOASIE: adj. proud, conceited, ostentatious. Combination of English boastful and Yoruba bosi-proud and ostentatious

BOBO: fool.

BOONOONOONOUS: Meaning wonderful.

BOX: To smack or to hit in the face.

BRAA: from BREDDA; brother. BRAATA: a little extra; like the 13th cookie in a baker's dozen; or an extra helping of food. In musical shows it has come to be the encore.

BREDREN: one's fellow male Rastas

BRINDLE: to be angry

BRINKS : title given to a man who is supplying a woman with money

BUBU: fool.

BUCKY: home-made gun

BUD : bird.

BUFU-BUFU: fat, swollen, blubbery; too big; clumsy or lumbering.

BUGUYAGA: a sloppy, dirty person, like a bum or tramp.

BULL BUCKA: a bully

BULLA: a comon sugar and flour cookie or small round cake, sold everywhere in Jamaica.

BLOOD CLOT: curse word

BUCK UP: meet

BUMBO: bottom; backside. BUMBY: by-and-byBUNKS: to knock or bump against, from "to bounce",

BUNKS MI RES: catch my rest, take a nap.

BWOY: Boy

C

CALLALOU : A spinach stew.

CARD : to fool someone

CALABAN: - bird trap

CEASE & SEKKLE!: Stop everything and relax!

CEPES : (n.) beard

CERACE: a ubiquitous vine used for boiling medicinal tea, and for bathing. It is proverbial for its bitterness.

CHA! or CHO!: a disdainful expletive pshaw! very common, mild explanation expressing impatience, vexation or disappointment.

CHAKA-CHAKA: messy, disorderly, untidy.

CHANT : (v.) - to sing, especially cultural or spiritual songs

CHEAP: just as cheap, just as well.

CHIMMY: chamber pot.

CHO: very common, mild explanation expressing impatience, vexation or disappointment.

CLAP: hit, break, stride

CLOT: 1. cloth, an essential part of most Jamaican bad words, such as bumbo clot, rass clot, blood clot, etc. The essence of Jamaican cursing seems to be nastiness, rather than the blashemy or sexuality which is characteristic of the metropolitan countries; to hit or strike COCO: a potato-like edible root, known elsewhere as the taro or the eddo. It was brought to Jamaica from the South Pacific. This is completely distinct from cocoa, usually called chocolate.

COIL: money

COME DUNG: come down, get ready (as to prepare to play a tune)

COME EEN LIKE: to seem as if; to resemble.

CONTROL : to be in charge of, responsible for, to own; to take COO 'PON: v. (origin unclear) Look upon!

COO YAH: v. (origin unclear) Look here! pay attention

COOL RUNNINGS: usually used at a time of departure on a long journey meaning have a safe trip

COME YAH (cumyu) : come here.

CORK UP: jammed, filled, crowded

CORN: 1. marijuana 2. money 3. a bullet

COTCH: verb (cotch up), to support something else, as with a forked stick; to balance something or place it temporarily; to beg someone a cotch, can be a place on a crowded bus seat or bench; or it may mean to cotch a while, to stay somewhere temporarily.

COTTA: a roll of cloth or vegetation placed on top of the head to cushion the skull from the weight of a head load.

CRAB: aside from it's usual meaning, it is a verb meaning to scratch or claw.

CRAVEN: greedy

CRIS: crisp; popularly used for anything brand-new, slick-looking.

CRISSARS: crisp, brand-new

CROMANTY: adj. from Corromantee, Blacks from the Gold Coast believed to be rebellious

CROCUS BAG: a very large sack made of coarse cloth, like burlap

CROSSES: problems, vexations, trials; bad luck, misfortunes.

CRUCIAL: serious, great, "hard,", "dread"

CUBBITCH: covetous.

CUDJO: n. name of famous Maroon warrior; mn born on Monday, from Fante, Twi kudwo

CULTURE: reflecting or pertaining to the roots values and traditions highly respected by the Rastas

CUSS-CUSS: a quarrel or fracas, with lots of cursing.

CUT YAI: to cut your eye at somebody is a very common means of expressing scorn or contempt, for example; one catches the other person's eye, then deliberatly turns one's own eyes as an insult.

CYAAN: cannot, can't

D

D.J.: a person who sings or scats along with dub music, sometimes called "toasting"

DAAL: split peas, usually a thick soup, from Indian cuisine, from Hindi.

DADA: father

DALLY: executive zig-zag movements on wheels or on foot to ride a bicycle or motorbike with a weaving motion, as when ones weaves around potholes.

DAN DADA: the highest of DON'S

DAN: than

DARKERS: sunglasses

DASHEEN: a big soft yam-like root, often slightly greyish when cooked. It is related to the coco, but one eats the "head" instead of the tubers.

DAWTA: a girl, woman, "sister," girlfriend

DEAD WOOD: (the w is silent) = A man that can't perform sexually. Impotent.

DEADERS: meat, meat by-products

DEESTANT: decent. DEGE or DEGE-DEGE : adjective, little, skimpy, measly, only, as in a two dege-dege banana.

DEH: there (place)

DEY: v. to be, exist, as in "No yam no dey". From Ewe de or Twi de - to be

DEY 'PON : (aux. v.) - to be engaged in action or continuing activity

DI: the

DINKI: a kind of traditional dance at funerals or "nine nights" ("set-ups"); now popular among school children.

DIS or DIS YA: this

DJEW: as a verb, rain a djew; as a noun, djew rain. It means a light rain or drizzle.

DOGHEART: a person who is especially cold and cruel

DOLLY: executive zig-zag movements on wheels

DON: one who is respected, master of a situation

DONKYA: from "don't care"; careless, sloppy, lacking ambition, etc.

DOONDOOS: an albino.

DOWNPRESSOR: preferred term for oppressor

DOTI: earth

(TO) DRAW CARD: the act of fooling someone

DREAD: 1. a person with dreadlocks; 2. a serious idea or thing; 3. a dangerous situation or person; 4. the "dreadful power of the holy"; 5. experientially, "awesome, fearful confrontation of
a people with a primordial but historically denied racial selfhood"

DREADLOCKS: 1. hair that is neither combed nor cut; 2. a person with dreadlocks

DREADY: a friendly term for a fellow dread

DUB: a roots electronic music, created by skillful, artistic re-engineering of recorded tracks

DUCK-ANTS: white ants, or termites.

DUKUNU: sweet corn-meal dumplings boiled in wrapped leaves.

DUNDUS: an albino.

DUNGLE: n. legendary West Kingston slum surrounding a garbage dump, now cleared. : From English dunghill

DUNS, DUNSA: money

DUPPY: a ghost

DUTCHY: dutch cooking pot, low round-bottomed heavy pot.

E

EASE-UP: to forgive, to lighten up

EVERYTING COOK & CURRY: all is well, all is taken care of

F

FALLA FASHIN: Copycat

FAS': to be fast with, meaning to be rude, impertinent, to meddle with sombody's business, to be forward, etc.

FASSY: eczema-like scratchy sores on the skin; also a verb meaning to cause oneself to be covered with fassy by scratching.

FAASTIE: impertinent, rude, impudent

FAYVA: to favour, resemble, or look like; "fayva like" also means "it seems as if".

FE: the infinitive "to" as in "Have fe go": "a fe" Have to "fe dem" their FEEL NO WAY: don't take offense, don't be sorry, don't worry

FENKY-FENKY: (from finicky) choosy, proud, stuck-up.

FENNEH: v. to feel physical distress, pain. From Twi fene-to vomit; Fante fena-to be troubled; Lumba feno-to faint

FI: possessive. "fi me"-"mine" Can also mean: "for" or "to", as in "I ha' fi", I have to: Yu num fi du dat = You are not to do that.

FIESTY: impudent, rude, out of order, cheeky.

FIRST LIGHT: tomorrow

FIT: when used of fruits and vegetables, it means ready to pick, full grown, though not necessarily fully ripe. also means in good shape. ("You haffe fit!")

FORWARD: 1. to go, move on, set out 2. in the future

FULLNESS, TO THE FULLNESS : completely, absolutely, totally

FUNDS: Money

G

GAAN TO BED: an adverbial phrase; following a verb of liking or loving, it has a superlative meaning; Can be used in any context, such as "I love hafu yam gaan to bed!".

GALANG: go along.

GANJA: herb, marijuana

GANSEY: t-shirt, any knit shirt

(TO) GET SALT: to be thwarted, to encounter misfortune

GATES : home, yard

GENERAL: cool operator

GI: give

GIG: spinning top.

GINNAL: n. trickster, con-man, an Anancy figure as in "Sunday Ginnal"-a preacher or clergyman.

GORGON: outstanding dreadlocks

(DON) GORGON: outstanding dreadlocks, a person who is respected (2,6)

GRAVALICIOUS: greedy, avaricious.

GRINDSMAN: one who displays great prowess in bed

GROUND: home, yard

H

HACKLE: to hassle, bother, worry, trouble. As a noun, hackling.

HAFFI : to have to…

HAIL: a greeting

HARD: excellent, proficient, skillful, uncompromising

HARD EARS: stubborn, doesn't listen

HEETCH: itch. Many such words could be listed under H, as initial H is added to scores of words at will.

HEAD MAN JANCRO: n. albino buzzard

HIEZ-HAAD: ears-hard, thick skulled, stubborn, unwilling or unable to hear.

HIEZ: ears.

HIGGLERS: higglers, who are primarly woman who buy and sell goods that they have imported into the country. Some higglers, however, do not make trips out of the country to buy goods, but sell the goods that others import. The connection between higglers and dancehall culture is crucial as they form one of the strongest international links between JA, North America, and the Caribbean.

HITEY-TITEY: upper class, high tone, "stoosh".

HOMELY: to be relaxed, comfortable, enjoying your home surrounding.

HORTICAL (DON): respected, acclaimed

HOT-STEPPER: fugitive from jail or gun court

I

I-DREN: (n.)- male Rastafarian

I-MAN: I, me, mine

I-NEY: a greeting

I-REY: 1. a greeting 2. excellent, cool, highest

I-SHENCE: herb

I-TAL: vital, organic, natural, wholesome; refers to way of cooking and way of life in colors, red, green and gold

I: replaces "me", "you", "my"; replaces the first syllable of seleted words I and I, I&I: I, me, you and me, we Rastafari speech eliminates you, me we, they, etc., as divisive and replaces same with communal I and I. I and I embrace the congregation in unity with the Most I (high) in an endless circle of inity (unity).

IEZ-HAAD: ears-hard, thick skulled, stubborn, unwilling or unable to hear.

IEZ: ears.

ILIE: adj. literally, "highly", valuable, exalted, even sacred

IGNORANT: short-tempered, easy to vex, irate.

INNA DI MORROWS: tomorrow

INNA: In the

IRIE: A Greeting. excellent, cool, highest: adj. powerful and pleasing

ISES/IZES/ISIS: praises Praises to the almighty given by Rasta: when calling on the name of Jah for strength and: assistance for achieving progress in life.

ISMS and SKISMS: negative term denoting Babylon's classificatory systems

ITES: 1. the heights; 2. a greeting; 3. the color red great

J

JA, JAM-DOWN: Jamaica

JACKASS ROPE : homegrown tobacco, twisted into a rope.

JAH KNOW: Lord knows

JAH: God; possibly derived as a shortened form of Jahweh or Jehovah Jah Ras Tafari, Haille Selassie, King of Kings, Lord of Lords, conquering Lion of Judah; rastas revere Haile Selassie as the personification of the Almighty

JAMDUNG: Jamaica, "Jam" to press down "dung" down. Ironic reference to social and economic conditions of the masses

JAMMIN: to be having a good time, to be dancing calypso/soca

JANCRO: n. literally John Crow, buzzard

JANGA: shrimp, crayfish.

JELLY: a young coconut, full of jelly. JON CONNU: n . (John Canoe). Bands of elaborately masked dancers appearing around Christmas. They ressemble the ancestral dancers of West Africa, but the ety. of the word is unclear.

JOOK: to pierce or stick, as with a thorn or a long pointed stick.

JUDGIN': adjective, everyday or ordinary clothes or shoes worn in the yard or in the bush, as in "judgin' boot". Also as a verb, to judge, with a similar meaning.

JUMBE: evil spirit

JUU: as a verb, rain a juu; as a noun, juu rain. It means a light rain or drizzle.

K

KALLALOO: a dark, green leafy vegetable, very nutritious and cheap.

KASS KASS: n. quarrel or contention. From combination of English curse or cuss, and Twi kasa kasa-to dispute verbally

KATA: a roll of cloth or vegetation placed on top of the head to cushion the skull from the weight of a head load.

KAYA: see ganja

KETCH UP : grapple

KEMPS: a little bit, a tiny piece, from skimps.

KIN TEET : see kiss teet

KISS ME NECK!: common exclamation of surprise.

KISS TEET: to kiss one's teeth or to suck one's teeth is to make the very common hissing noise of disappoval, dislike, vexation or disappointment.

KOUCHIE: bowl of a chalice or chillum pipe

KRENG-KRENG: an old-fashioned meat rack, hung up high over the fire to catch the smoke.

KU : verb, look!

KU DEH!: look there!

KU PAN: look at.

KU YA!: look here!

KU YU : To say "Look at you." To the person you are refering to.

KUMINA: n. Ecstatic dance for the purpose of communicating with ancestors. From Twi akom-to be possessed and ana-by an ancestor

KYA: 1. to care; "donkya", don't care, careless; "no kya" means no matter, as in "no kya weh im tun", no matter where he turns; 2. to carry.

KYAAN: can't.

KYAI: to carry.

KYAN: can.

L

LABA-LABA: to chat, gab; gossip.

LABRISH: gossip, chit-chat.

LAGGA HEAD: Dumb acts as if you have no common sense. Stupid. LARGE: respected

LET OFF: pay out

LEGGO BEAS' : wild, disorderly, like a let-go beast.

LICK: To hit LICKY-LICKY: fawning, flattering, obsequious.

LILLY BIT: little bit, tiny.

LION: a righteous Dread a great soul

LITTLE MORE: see you later

(TOO) LIKKY-LIKKY : title given to those who like to eat any food they encounter, without discretion

M

MAAS: n. from master or massa. Now freed from its class origin; a respectful form of address to an older man; chill out, be by ones self for a while

MACA: thorn, prickle.

MADDA: mother

MAFIA: big-time criminals

MAGA DOG: mongrel

MAGA: thin (from meagre)

MAMPI: Fat or overweight

MANACLES: chains

MANNERS: under heavy discipline or punishment. for example when Kingston is under "heavy manners", they have a curfew or call out the army.

MARINA: a man's undershirt, guernsey; a tank-top style.

MAROON: n. free black warrior-communities which successfully resisted British hegemony during eighteenth century and early nineteenth century. From Spanish cimmaron- untamed, wild

MASCOT: denoting inferior status

MASH IT UP: a huge success

MASH UP, MASH DOWN: destroy

MASSIVE: respected, used with LARGE to add emphasis

MATEY: mistress

MEK WE: Let Us.

MENELIK, RAS: n. Ethiopian nobleman who rallied his troops to resist Italian aggression. Defeated Italians at Adowa 1896

MONKS: amongst.

MORE TIME: see you later

MR. MENTION: Talk of the town, originally talk of the females signifying someone with many female conquests

MR. T: the boss

MUS MUS: a rat

MY BABY MOTHER/FATHER: the mother/father of my child

MYAL: n. a form of benign magic oposed to Obeah, hence myalman. From Hursa maye-wizard, person of mystic power.

N
NAGAH: n. pejorative for a black person
NAGO: n. Yoruba person, practice or language. From Ewe anago-Yoruba person
NAH: adv. will not. Emphatic as in "Me nah do that"
NANA: midwife; nanny or nurse.
NANNY GOAT: "What sweet nanny goat a go run him belly" is a cautionary Jamaican proverb which translated means: What tastes good to a goat will ruin his belly. In other words - the things that seem good to you now, can hurt you later…
NATTY, NATTY DREAD,
NATTY CONGO: 1. dreadlocks 2. a person with dreadlocks
NAZARITE: Ancient Hebrew meaning to "separate", conse-crated, set apart by choice and devotion NIYABINGHI: 1. "death to all black and white oppressors"; 2. East African warriors who resisted colonial domination; 3. large Rastafarian meeting and spiritual gathering; 4. referring to orthodox, traditional Rastas; 5. a variety of drumming
NIYAMEN: name for Rastas referring to Niyabinghi warriors of East Africa
NO KYA: no matter, as in "no kya weh im tun", no matter where he turns.
NO TRUE?: isn't it so?
NOTCH : Don or top ranking badman
NUH: interrogative at end of sentence; literally, "Is it not so?"
NYAM: to eat.
(TOO) NYAMI-NYAMI : title given to those who like to eat any food they encounter, without discretion
NYING'I-NYING'I: nagging, whining.

O

O-DOKONO : boiled maize bread.

OBEAH: traditional African "science", relating to matters of the spirit and spirits, spells, divinations, omens, extra-sensory knowledge, etc.

OHT FI: about to, on the vergeof, as in "it hoht fi rain", it is about to rain, it looks like rain.

ONE LOVE: a parting phrase, expression of unity

ONE-ONE: adjective, one by one, thus any small amount.

ONGLE: only.

P

PAKI: calabash, gourd.

PAPAA: pawpaw, or papaya melon.

PATTAN: pattern, style and fashion

PATU: owl.

PAYAKA: heathen

PYAKA: tricky or dishonest.

PEEL-HEAD: bald-headed, usually certain chickens or vultures.

PEENYWALLY: a kind of large fire fly, actually a type of flying beetle.

PEER: avocado pear.

PHENSIC: Jamaican equivalent to Tylenol, Excedrin, etc.

PICKY, PICKY HEAD : brush haircut

PICKY-PICKY: 1. finicky or choosy; 2. Used of uncombed hair just starting to turn into dreadlocks.

PIKNY: pickaninny, child. PINDA: peanut.

PIRA: a low wooden stool.

PITY-ME-LIKL : a type of very tiny red ant whose bite is so hot and long-lasting it resembles a sting.

POCOMANIA, POCO: Christian revival, distinct drum rhythm

POLYTRICKS: politics (by Peter Tosh)

POLYTRICKSTERS: politicians (by Peter Tosh)

POPPY-SHOW: from puppet show, it is used in the idiom, tek smadi mek poppy-show, which means to make fun of someone or shame them, making them look ridiculous.

PUPPALICK: somersalt.

PUTTIN' AWAY: a preposition, meaning "except for", or "except".

PYAA-PYAA: sickly, weak; feeble, of no account.

PYU: from spew; verb used of running sores or anything similarly dripping or oozing.

Q

QUASHIE: n. peasant, country bumpkin, coarse and stupid person; racial pejorative generic term for blacks; originally Twi name of a boy born on a Sunday

QUATTIE: penny ha'penny

QUIPS: 1. nouns (from squips) a tiny piece or amount; 2. verb, the Jamaican art of washing clothes making a "squips-squips" sound.

QUI-QUI: squeaky

R

RAATID!: a common mild expletive of surprise or vexation, as in "to raatid!". It is likely a polite permutation of "ras", a la "gosh" or "heck".

RAM : full up

RAM GOAT : slang for someone who deals with nuff ladies

RANKING: highly respected

RAS or RASS: backside, rump; a common curse is to rass! or rass clot! a title used by Rastafarians meaning "lord" or "head" .

(TO) RAAS: "really?", "damn!"

RASTA, RASTAFARIAN: a follower of Marcus Garvey who worships the Almighty in the person of haile Selassie

RAT-BAT: bat, the night-flying rodent.

RATCHET: a switchblade knife popular in Jamaica

RED: 1. very high on herb 2. mulatto color

RED EYE: to want another persons belonging, envious. "You too red eye": meaning, you're too envious.

RAHTID: expression of surprise, or to be enraged. From biblical"wrothed"

RENK: 1. foul-smelling, raw-smelling; 2. out of order, impudent, as in a rank-imposter. "Yu too renk!".

RHYGIN: adj. spirited, vigorous, lively, passionate with great vitality and force; also sexually provocative and aggressive. Probably a form of English raging.

RIZZLA: brand of rolling paper.

ROCKERS: reggae music reggae music as it is played today, the latest sound ROOTS: 1. derived from the experience of the common people, natural indigenous; 2. a greeting; 3. name for a fellow Rasta

ROTI: flat Indian pan breads.

ROYAL, (RIAL): n. offspring of some other race and black, ass in "Chiney-Rial," "coolie-rial"; humorous as in "monkey-rial"

RUDE BOY: a criminal, a hard hearted person, a tough guy

RUN-DUNG: food cooked in coconut juice, obtained after grating the dry coconut meat and squeezing it in water, thus extracting the coconut cream.

RUNNING BELLY: diarrhea

RYAL: royal.

S

SAL'TING: 1. dishes cooked with saltfish or meat; 2. that part of the meal which is served with the "food" (starchy food, ground food); 3. by some strange extension, the female organ, often
simply called "sal".

SALT: adjective, broke, empty-handed, low on funds or food, as in "tings salt" or "i' salt".

SAMBO: the colour between brown and black; someone who is a cross between a mullatto (brown) and a black.

SAMFAI MAN: trickster, conman.

SHAMPATA: n. sandal of wood or tire rubber. Span. zapato

SANFI : A manipulator - dishonest person. A person that will sweet talk you: out of love and money.

SANKEY: n. religious song of a paticularly lugubrious tone, sung in the long or common meter. From Ira David Sankey, evangelist and hymnalist

SATA: to rejoice, to meditate, to give thanks and praise.

SATTA: sit, rest, meditate relax

(GO) SATTA: claim how spiritual you are

SCIENCE: obeah, witchcraft

SCIENTIST: occult practitioner

SCOUT: denoting inferior status

SCREECHIE: to sneak by

SCREW: to scowl, to be angry

SEEN: I understand, I agree

SEEN?: Do you understand?

SHAG: home-cured tobacco, straight from the field.

SHAKE OUT: leave without haste, casually

SHEG (UP): verb, to bother, as in "all sheg up", all hot and bothered, or or spoiled up (as of work).

SHEG-UP: to be messed up, ruined

SHEPHERD: n. leader of revivalist cult; also proprietor of balmyard, healer and prophet

SHOOB: to shove.

SIDUNG: sit down

SIGHT?: do you understand?

SINKL-BIBLE: the aloevera plant.

SINSEMILLA, SENSIE: popular, potent, seedless, unpollinated female strain of marijuana SINTING: something.

SIPPLE: slippery; slimy.

SISTER, SISTREN: a woman, a friend, woman Rastafarians SITTIN': something.

SKANK: to dance to reggae music to move with cunning, ulterior motives
SKIL: kiln, as in "limeskil".
SKIN YOUR TEETH: smile
SLABBA-SLABBA: big and fat, slobby, droopy.
SLACKNESS: lewd, vulgar lyrics popular in DJ singing
SMADI: somebody.
SO-SO: only, solely, unaccompanied. weak, pallid
SOFT: not well done, amateurish; unable to cope broke, no money
SPRING: to sprout, as of yams or cocos, making them inedible.
STAR: common term of affection, camaraderie
STEP: to leave, to depart briskly, quickly
STOOSH/STOSHUS: upper class, high tone, "hitey-titey".
STRING UP: a muscial rehearsal
STRUCTURE: body, health
SU-SU: gossip, the sound of wispering.
SUFFERER: a poor person stuggling to survive
SUPM, SINTING: something

T
TACK: bullet
TACUMAH: n. character in Anancy tales. Said to be the son of Anancy. Twin'ticuma
TAKARI/TANKARI: stewed spicy pumpkin.
TALL: long
TALLOWAH: adj. sturdy, strong, fearless, physically capable. From Ewe talala
TAM: deep woolen hat, used by Dreads to cover their locks
TAMBRAN SWITCH: n. a flail made from the wiry branches of the Tamarind tree, braided and oiled. Effective and much feared in the hands of Babylon.

TAN': to stand; usually used in the sense of "to be". "A so im tan", "that is what he is like"; "tan deh!" or "yu tan deh!" means "just you wait!". "Tan tedy", stand steady, means "hold still".

TARRA-WARRA: a polite way of expressing omitted bad words, a verbal asterisk.

TATA: n. father. Affectionate and respectful title for an old man. Fram many african languages. Ewe, Ge, N'gombe

TATU: a little thatched hut, often made of bamboo.

TEETH: bullets

TEIF: a theif, to steal

THE I : (pron.) -you, yourself, yours

THRU' : because

TOAST : (v.) - to rap or sing spontaneously over a dub track

TOTO: coconut cake.

TOPANORIS: uptown snobby person.

TRACE: to curse or speak abusively to someone. TRANSPORT: vehicle

TUMPA: from stump, as in "tumpa-foot man", a one-foot man.

U

UNO/UNU: you-all. pron. you, plural. In usage close to Afro-American y'awl. From Ibo unu, same meaning

UPFUL: postitive, encouraging

UPHILL: positive, righteous

UPTOWN: the upper classes

V

VANK: (v.) - to vanquish, conquer

VEX: to get angry

W

WA DAY: adverbial phrase, the other day.

WA MEK?: why?

WHAFEDOO: we'll have to (make) do or we'll have to deal with it.

WAKL: wattle, a kind of woven bamboo work used to make house walls.

WANGA-GUT: hungry-belly.

WARRA-WARRA: politely omitted bad words, same as "tarra-warra".

WENCHMAN: a kind of fish, "hail brother john, have you any wenchman?" (from "Row Fisherman Row").

WH'APPEN?: what's happening?

WHATLEF: What's left over?

WHEELS: vehicle

WHOLE HEAP: a lot

WINE: "wine" appears in every West Indian dialect, and is literally a corruption of "wind." It means to dance, sometimes seductively.

WINJY: thin and sickly looking.

WIS: vine, liana, from withe.

WOLF: a non-rasta deadlocks

Y

YA NO SEE IT?: you know?

YA: hear, or here.

YABBA: a big clay pot.

YAGA YAGA: Dancehall slang. a way to big up a brethren; to express a greeting or attract attention, i.e. yo! or yush! true friend; bonafide; brethren.

YAHSO: here (place)

YAI: eye.

YARD: home, one's gates tenement

YOUTH: a child, a young man, an immature man YUSH: Yush talk is bad boy talk. Or it can be a way of saying "YO". In other words it is a way for rude boys to hail each other up.

Z

ZION: Ethiopia, Africa, the Rastafarian holy land
ZUNGU PAN: zinc pan.

Jamaican Proverb Answers

1. full.
2. mek.
3. kill.
4. hawk.
5. four
6. wanti.
7. bite.
8. who.
9. another.
10. faster.
11. bus
12. ketch
13. blind
14. get
15. fowl.
16. counter.
17. cold.
18. nyam.
19. fleas.
20. taste.

Some Traditional Jamaican Foods and Recipes

All these recipes come from my church sisters and brothers and are tried and true! How I started making these Jamaican dishes was for various church fundraising project over the years when I was ministering with them. We would set up a cook drum outside in the church parking lot and BBQ Jerk chicken, Jerk pork, roasted corn on the cob and rice and peas. I would make my secret jerk sauce for the meat and rice. One of my church sisters would make Akee and Saltfish, baked fish and oxtail, curry goat, fried bananas, seamed cabbage and it was all so delicious! We would eat it with hard dough bread and dumplings with gusto. We always washed it all down with coconut water and ginger ale while we played Caribbean Gospel music from a local radio program on WVKR 91.3 FM. KoolMeditations, hosted by my friend Christine Williams on Saturdays. As the smoke thickened and bellowed down the road, people would pass by with their cars and have to turn around just for a little bit of our taste of heaven and had a real fun time fellowshipping with the Lord! One Love!

Enjoy!

Ackee and Saltfish - The Jamaica National Dish

INGREDIENTS:
1/2 lb. Saltfish (codfish)
1 dozen ackees
1 small onion
1 teaspoon black pepper
3 slices hot scotch bonnet pepper
1 small red sweet pepper
cooking oil

METHOD:
1. Soak Saltfish in warm water to taste.
2. After soaking saltfish (codfish), place it in cold water and boil.
3. Clean the achee. Remove the seeds and all traces of interior red pit from the ackees.
4. Wash ackees five times
5. Cover and boil until moderately soft.
6. Drain, cover, and put aside.
7. Pick up (flake) the saltfish and remove all bones.
8. Sauté thinly sliced onions and sweet pepper rings.
9. Remove half of the fried onions and peppers
10. Add saltfish and the ackees, and turn the fire/stove up slightly.
11. Add black pepper
12. Pour in to serving plate and garnish with remaining onions and pepper slices

Ackee

This fruit is native to tropical West Africa. Ackee is one of the most preferred choices of food in Jamaica. Even though ackee is regarded as a fruit, Jamaicans often consider it to be a kind of meat that can be served with a staple or carbohydrate. Ackee is the national fruit of Jamaica, and ackee and saltfish is the national dish. Ackee can also be prepared with a variety of meat kinds, some of which include sardine, mackerel, red herring, corned pork, and chicken.

Ackee is the national fruit of Jamaica and is in clusters on an evergreen tree. Ackee trees are found across the island of Jamaica but the main producing areas are located in Clarendon and St Elizabeth. There are two bearing seasons: between January to March and June to August.

Warning: Only eat ripe or canned ackee. Do not eat the unripe fruit because you can suffer from 'Jamaican vomiting sickness" JVS, which has resulted in some fatalities in the past. Symptoms are vomiting and severe hypoglycemia. Diagnosed patients generally show manifestations of chronic malnutrition and vitamin deficiency.

Jamaican Grilled Fish

INGREDIENTS:
3 Medium Snappers (or any in season)
Salt to taste
Pepper to Taste
Powder Onion
Pimento (all spice) branches or aromatic wood
Red Stripe Beer and Water
Lemon

METHOD:
1. Cut fish in slices and add salt, pepper, powdered onion and pimento
2. Squeeze lemon over the fish
3. Marinate for about 2 hours in the refrigerator.
4. Mix a solution of half water and half beer (salt is optional)
5. Grill the fish on a low fire.
6. Sprinkle the fish occasionally with Beer/water solution to keep it moist and keep the fire low.
7. Cook for approximately 25-35 minutes
8. Serve with 4

Tips on Grilling Seafood

A hinged wire grill basket is best for cooking whole fish such as snapper, trout or salmon. It also works well for fillets of tender fish such as perch, snapper, catfish or flounder.

Firm fish, such as tuna, salmon, or shark can be cooked directly on the grill if handled carefully. Skewer small shellfish such as shrimp or scallops on metal or water-soaked wooden skewers or cook them in a grill basket.

Grill fillets over medium to medium-low heat. Fish can cook quickly and it is easier to slow down cook time and monitor to not overcook.

Turn fish only once. (Flipping back and forth will break fish apart.)

If using a marinade, allow fish to soak up flavor for at least 30 minutes. Refrigerate while w soaking in marinade.

If you are going to use the marinade as an extra sauce on top of the cooked fish or seafood, the marinade liquid must be boiled by itself for at least 5 minutes to cook out any bacteria that may be there from when the fish was soaking in the marinade.

If you are going to use the marinade as an extra sauce on top of the cooked fish or seafood, the marinade liquid must be boiled by itself for at least 5 minutes to cook out any bacteria that may be there from when the fish was soaking.

To grill shellfish in the shell, such as oysters, mussels and clams, place them directly on the hottest part of the grill. They're done when the shell opens. Discard those that don't open after about 5 minutes.

Jerk Chicken

2- 3 1/2- to 4-pound chickens, quartered, or 8 whole legs, or 5 to 6 pounds bone-in, skin-on thighs.

Wash chicken in a mix of vinegar and lemon juice.

Time: About 1 1/2 hours, plus at least 12 hours' marinating

Jerk Seasoning Ingredients:
1 large bunch scallions, white and green parts
2 shallots, peeled and halved
4 to 6 Scotch bonnet chili peppers, stems removed, or habaneras
1 2-inch piece fresh ginger, peeled and coarsely chopped
6 garlic cloves, peeled
1/4 cup fresh thyme leaves, or 1 tablespoon dried
2 tablespoons ground allspice, more for sprinkling
2 tablespoons soy sauce
2 tablespoons dark brown sugar
1 tablespoon salt, more for sprinkling
1 tablespoon black pepper
1/2 cup vegetable oil
1 tablespoon white or apple cider vinegar
Freshly squeezed juice of 2 limes

METHOD:
1. At least 1 day before cooking, pat chicken dry with paper towels. Combine remaining ingredients in a blender or food

processor and grind to a coarse paste. Slather all over chicken, including under skin. Refrigerate 12 to 36 hours. Bring to room temperature before cooking and lightly sprinkle with more salt and ground allspice.

2. Prepare a charcoal grill: Clean and oil grates, and preheat to medium heat using one chimney of charcoal. The temperature can start as high as 300 degrees and go as low as 250. For best results, coals should be at least 12 inches away from chicken. If necessary, push coals to one side of grill to create indirect heat. Add two large handfuls of soaked pimento (allspice) wood sticks and chips (see note) or other aromatic wood chips to coals, then close grill. When thick white smoke billows from grill, place chicken on grate, skin side up, and cover. Let cook undisturbed for 30 to 35 minutes.

3. Uncover grill. Chicken will be golden and mahogany in places. Chicken thighs may already be cooked through. For other cuts, turn chicken over and add more wood chips, and charcoal if needed. Cover and continue cooking, checking and turning every 10 minutes. Jerk chicken is done when skin is burnished brown and chicken juices are completely clear, with no pink near the bone. For large pieces, this can take up to an hour. Serve hot or warm, with rice and beans.

Variations: If you have no grill, chicken can be baked in oven at 375 degrees for about 45 minutes; the smokiness will be lost but seasoning will be intact. Jerk rub can be used on a boneless leg of lamb or pork roast, to be cooked on a medium-hot grill or in oven.

Jerk Pork: The pieces are large and succulent, rimmed with fat, and slightly gritty with generous quantities of jerk spices and oven bake.

Charcoal: Plain hardwood charcoal, showered during the cooking with handfuls of Pimento allspice berries, "If the smoke is so thick outside that you can't see, that's a good sign."

Jerk Sauce: Jerk Seasonings, Scotch Bonnets, Ketchup, BBQ sauce, Water Mixed together. Most local jerk is made mild, with hot sauce put on afterward.

Jerk Style

Jerk is a style of cooking native to Jamaica in which meats are dry-rubbed or marinated with a very hot spice mixture called Jamaican jerk spice. Jerk seasoning is traditionally applied to pork and chicken. Today you can jerk anything including tofu, and vegetables.

Modern recipes also apply Jerk spice mixes to fish, shellfish, beef, sausage, and tofu. Jerk seasoning principally relies upon two items: allspice which is called "pimento" in Jamaica and Scotch bonnet peppers which is among the hottest peppers on the Scoville heat unit in the world of hot sauce.

Other ingredients include cloves, cinnamon, scallions, nutmeg, thyme, and garlic. Jerk chicken, pork, or fish tastes excellent when smoked over aromatic wood charcoal or briquettes. The "Pimento wood" berries, and leaves of the allspice plant mixed among the coals contribute to jerk's distinctive flavor.

In many indigenous cultures throughout the Americas, and especially in the Caribbean, jerk meat was a primary method of protein preservation. By cutting game and fish into strips and drying it in the sun for use at a later date, many native peoples of the Americas and the Caribbean were able to retain valuable meat for leaner times.

Curry Goat

INGREDIENTS :
3 lb. goat
3-4 tablespoon curry
2 onion,
4 stalks thyme
2 stalks garlic
2 Whole Scotch Bonnet pepper
black pepper and salt
2 Small carrots cut in slices (Optional)

METHOD:
1. Wash & season with curry, thyme, garlic, black peppers & salt, onions
2. For best results let seared meat sit overnight in refrigerator
3. Pour a little oil in pot and heat
4. Please meat in pot and let brown a little
5. Add 1 cup water and seasoning
6. Add Carrots (Optional)
7. Cook until tender
8. Add whole scotch bonnet pepper for flavor and simmer for minutes
9. Make gravy by adding a teaspoon corn starch
10. Serve with white rice

Curry Goat Origins

Curry goat is a dish originating in Indo-Jamaican cuisine that has become so popular it is now regarded as being typical of Jamaica and goat, is so common that a party without this delicious, juicy, succulent meat would be a waste of time.

Curry goat is a popular party dish in Jamaica and at a 'big dance' a local expert or 'specialist' is often brought in to cook it.

Goat basically tastes like lamb, but is far leaner. Lamb is the fattiest of the red meats. It's very popular in a variety of ethnic cuisines, but for some reason has yet to gain a real following in the US.

Goat can be cooked in many different ways. You can stew, barbecue, roast, kebob, pot roast, etc, but the one popular style of cooking goat in the Caribbean is Curry Goat.

Bully Beef

INGREDIENTS :
1 can of corned beef
1 medium onion (sliced)
2 sprigs fresh thyme
1 medium ripe tomato (chopped)
2 stalks scallion (chopped)
1 scotch bonnet pepper (de-seed and chopped)
1 tablespoon vegetable oil or coconut oil
1 teaspoon of browning (optional)

METHOD:
1. Heat oil in a heavy bottomed frying pan (skillet) over moderate heat.
2. Add onions, garlic (optional) and scotch bonnet to frying pan. Sauté for approx 1-2 minutes.
3. Add thyme and corned beef. Turn down heat to medium- low and stir until cooked.
4. Add onions, garlic and chopped scotch bonnet in frying pan
5. Add chopped tomatoes, scallions, and browning (optional), stir well and cook for another 3 minutes. Use paper towels to absorb the extra vegetable oil, if any.
6. Bully Beef is usually served for breakfast with Johnny Cakes, boiled green bananas or toast. It can also be served with white rice.(Serves 4)

History of Corned Beef

Tinned corned beef often shortened to bully. Beef cured or pickled in brine. It is known as the Poor Man's Meal. The term "Corned" comes from putting meat in a large crock and covering it with large rock-salt kernels of salt that were referred to as "corns of salt" which looked like seeds and this preserved the meat.

The term Corned has been in the Oxford English Dictionary as early as 888 AD. The area of Cork, Ireland was a great producer of Corned Beef in the 1600's until 1825. It was their chief export and sent it all over the world, mostly in cans. The British army was sustained on cans of Cork's corned beef during the Napoleonic Wars and from the Boer War to WW2.

Homes in the Caribbean Islands had no refrigeration and corned beef was easily incorporated into recipes. Bully Beef is served for breakfast with Johnny Cakes, boiled green bananas or white rice.

The Bully Beef Jam-Witch is a popular sandwich that can be served as an appetizer on white hard dough bread with onions, sweet peppers and ketchup.

Jamaican Rice with Coconut and Red Beans

"Rice and Peas"

Time: 40 minutes

2 teaspoons vegetable oil
1 garlic clove, minced
1 scallion, including green parts, thinly sliced
2 cups uncooked white rice
1 14-ounce can coconut milk, well shaken
1 sprig fresh thyme
1 whole Scotch bonnet chili pepper (optional)
About 3 cups cooked small red beans or pinto beans (start with 1 1/2 cups dried beans or use 2 15-ounce cans, drained)
Pinch salt
Freshly ground black pepper

METHOD:
1. In a heavy saucepan with a tight-fitting lid, heat oil over medium heat. Add garlic and scallion and cook, stirring, just until softened, about 3 minutes; reduce heat if necessary to prevent browning.

2. Add rice, coconut milk, 1 cup water, thyme, Scotch bonnet if using, beans and salt. Bring to a boil over high heat, then stir well, reduce heat to very low, cover tightly and cook without disturbing for about 25 minutes, until liquid has been absorbed and rice is very tender. Add black pepper and more salt, if desired. Fluff before serving.

Yield: 8 servings.

Coconut

Coconut Milk

Coconut milk is made by simmering equal parts water and shredded coconut meat, then squeezing and straining the thick liquid remaining.

Coconut Cream

Is very similar to coconut milk but contains less water. The difference is mainly consistency. It has a thicker, more paste-like consistency, while coconut milk is generally a liquid. Coconut cream is used as an ingredient in cooking, having a mild non-sweet taste.

Coconut Water

The clear liquid inside young coconuts also called coconut juice. Fresh coconuts for drinking are typically harvested off the tree while they are green. Coconut Water has been heralded for its great health and healing benefits and is called the "Dew from Heaven."

Callaloo

INGREDIENTS :
1 lb. callaloo
1 tablespoon margarine
1 scotch bonnet pepper
1 medium chopped onion
black pepper
salt to taste
1/4 cup water

METHOD:
1. Wash callaloo leaves
2. Cut up callaloo leaves in pieces.
3. Sauté onion in margarine.
4. Add cut up callaloo leaves, water and stir.
5. Cover saucepan and cook callalloo are tender.
6. Add whole scotch bonnet pepper
7. Sprinkle with pepper and salt.
8. Simmer then serve with avocado pear.

Callaloo Greens

Pick healthy green dasheen leaves with a large purple dot. Because the leaf vegetable is used in some regions it may be locally called "callaloo" or "callaloo bush. You can substitute other related varieties, another callaloo-named green called Chinese spinach or Indian kale, ordinary spinach, Swiss chard, or even wild greens like tender lamb's quarters or delicate French sorrel. Spelled half a dozen different ways, this colorful word turns up in Jamaican records as early as 1696. This leafy, spinach-like vegetable is typically prepared as one would prepare turnip or collard greens.

Callaloo Gumbo

The Caribbean version of gumbo and comes out of Africa with a history as rich as the dish itself; and in the Caribbean the callaloo dish is very popular in Jamaica. It is almost always made with okra and dasheen or water spinach (Ipomoea aquatic). There are many variations of callaloo which may include coconut milk, crab, conch, Caribbean lobster, meats, chili peppers, and other seasonings such as chopped onions and garlic. The ingredients are added and simmered down to a stew-like consistency. When done, callaloo is dark green in color and is served as a side dish which may be used as gravy for other food.

Jamaican Steamed Cabbage

INGREDIENTS :
1- Medium cabbage
2- large carrots 2tablespoon margarine
1- teaspoon pepper flakes
2- sprig thyme
1- crushed garlic or 2 teaspoons garlic powder
2- or 3 small slices of a sweet green pepper.
1- medium chopped onion
black pepper & salt to taste
1/4 cup water

METHOD:
1. Wash cabbage
2. Cut up/slice cabbage leaves in pieces.
3. Sauté onion, garlic, pepper, thyme in margarine.
4. Add cut up cabbage water and stir.
5. Cover saucepan and cook until cabbage is tender.
6. Add pepper flakes
7. Sprinkle with pepper and salt.
8. Simmer then serve.

Avocados

In Jamaica, avocados are often eaten with bread, especially hard dough bread, with bullas (a round basic firm sweet cake, in which stale bread is often an ingredient), in vegetable salads, and as a side dish with meals. When eaten with bread and bulla avocados function as cheese or butter. When eaten in a salad or as a side dish avocados are treated as a vegetable. In some other places, avocados are often treated as fruits and are often used in drinks.

Try the following recipe: scoop out the flesh of one or two very well ripened avocados, purce it in a blender, add sweetened condensed milk to taste, and dilute as necessary with either water or cow's milk. It makes an excellent shake. Seasonings such as nutmeg and or vanilla may be added sparingly. And the undiluted mixture can be processed in an ice cream maker to make an interesting ice cream.

Citrus Curry Rice Salad

INGREDIENTS:
1 can or fresh mandarin oranges (10 oz)
1 cup water
1/4cup raisins
1/4 tsp salt
1/4 tsp pepper
1/4 tsp dried tarragon
1 ½ cup instant brown rice
1 cucumber, peeled, seeded & chopped
1/4 cup sliced celery
1/4 cup sliced green onion
1/4 cup chopped pecans (can be toasted)
1/4 cup plain non-fat yogurt

METHOD:
1. Drain oranges, reserving juice.
2. Mix juice, water, raisins and spices in a saucepan. Bring to a boil. Stir in rice.
3. Return to boil.
4. Reduce heat to low and cover and simmer for 5 minutes.
5. Remove from heat. Let stand for 5 minutes.
6. Spread in shallow pan. Freeze for 10 minutes (to quickly cool rice: .
7. Toss with remaining ingredients. Serves 6-8.

Curry

Blend of ground spices adapted by British settlers in India from the traditional spice mixtures of Indian cuisine; also, any dish characterized by such seasoning.

The basic ingredients of commercial curry powder are turmeric (which imparts the characteristic yellow color), cumin, coriander, and red, or cayenne, pepper. Other ingredients may include chilies, cloves, cinnamon, fenugreek, nutmeg, ginger, mace, mustard seed, fennel, poppy seed, allspice, anise, bay leaves, and black or white pepper, all roasted and ground fine.

Jamaican Patties

A Jamaican patty is a pastry that contains various fillings and spices baked inside a flaky shell, often tinted golden yellow with an egg yolk mixture or turmeric. It is made like a turnover but is more savory.

As its name suggests, it is commonly found in Jamaica, and is also eaten in other areas of the Caribbean.

It is traditionally filled with seasoned ground beef, but fillings can include chicken, vegetables, shrimp, lobster, fish, soy, ackee, mixed vegetables or cheese.

Gungo Peas Patties (Vegetarian)

INGREDIENTS :
½ pint green gungo peas
2 medium sized chopped onion
1 clove garlic
1 scotch bonnet hot pepper (Optional Only for a spicy version)
1 tablespoon black pepper
Salt for taste
3 slices bread
2 teaspoons cooking oil
1 ounce vegetable margarinc
1 cup water

METHOD:
1. Soak peas
2. Sauté chopped onion, pepper & garlic in oil
3. Soften bread with a little water & mash into soft pulp
4. Add peas bread, margarine & seasoning.
5. Cook for 20 minutes
6. When cool use as a fill for patty pastry

Pigeon Pea, Gungo Pea or GooGoo Beans in Jamaica

The cultivation of the pigeon pea goes back at least 3000 years. The centre of origin is most likely Asia, from where it travelled to East Africa and by means of the slave trade to the American continent. Today pigeon peas are widely cultivated in all tropical and semi-tropical regions of both the Old and the New World.

Pigeon peas grow well in hot climates, making them especially popular in the Caribbean and India. They have been cultivated throughout the tropics for centuries. The pigeon pea is a small, round, tan-colored seed with a pungent flavor and a mealy texture. It is sometimes mistaken for the black gram or mung bean. The ripe seeds are often ground into a meal, then mixed with palm oil, salt, and condiments; but Europeans use the young seeds like peas and the pods as a vegetable.

Jamaican Beef Patties

INGREDIENTS FOR BEEF FILLING:
2 lbs ground beef
8 sprigs of thyme
2 -4 scallions
2 small hot peppers
1 teaspoon paprika
half a loaf French bread
1 teaspoon salt

METHOD:
1. Grind scallion and hot peppers in a mincing mill.
2. Add to ground beef with salt.
3. Place meat in a saucepan making a well in the center into which place 4sprigs of thyme.
4. Cook without adding any water or fat until meat has lost its broth and only certain amount of oil remains.
5. Pour off excess oil and add this to the paprika to be used later on, strained for coloring meat.
6. While meat is being cooked, pour sufficient cold water over bread in a saucepan to cover and soak for a few minutes, then squeeze dry, saving water.
7. Pass bread through mincing mill and return the ground bread water with 4 sprigs of thyme and cook until bread is dry.
8. Combine meat and cooked bread.
9. Add color, paprika in sufficient quantity to color the meat to taste.
10. Cook together for a further 20 minutes.
11. Remove from fire. Cool for filling pastry circles.

INGREDIENTS FOR PASTRY:
11 ounces vegetable shortening
4 cups flour
1 level teaspoon salt
2/3 cup ice cold water

METHOD:
1. Trim all skin and fatty membrane from suet and set overnight in freezer.

2. Next day, with a very sharp knife shave suet as finely as possible.

3. Combine salt and flour, then work in suet as you would shortening in plain pastry, cutting it in with two knives.

4. Add iced water in sufficient amount so the dough can be rolled out.

5. Form into a ball and with a rolling pin, pat gently, turning the dough over once or twice in order to have it all properly held together.

6. Set overnight wrapped in wax paper and place in the freezer.

7. Next day, pull off enough dough (after defrosting) to roll into a circle the size of a breakfast saucer.

8. Dip dough in flour before rolling.

9. Roll quite thin and cut in a circle. (use saucer for help) In the center of each circle place a spoonful of meat, fold dough over to form a crescent shape seal edges with egg white or by crimping the edge and folding dough slightly under.

10. Do not prick the pastry.

11. Bake on ungreased tin sheet in a hot oven for about 35 minutes

12. This recipe will make about 3 dozen regular patties. If cocktail patties are needed, use a smaller cutter than a saucer.

13. Serving 3 dozen regular size patties. Try different fillings for experiment.

Fried Green Plantains

INGREDIENTS :
2 green plantains
1 tablespoon salt

METHOD:
1. Peel plantain by making 2 incisions on opposite sides of the plantain skin.
2. Please save the skin and try not to break it.
3. Lay the plantain on a cutting board & cut the plantain into 1 inch slices in the middle (width, not length - like breaking a banana in 2).
4. Heat skillet filled with just enough oil to cover the 1 inch slices.
5. Fry plantain slices until golden brown on each side.
6. Each slice needs about 30 seconds to cook.
7. Remove them a slice at a time, then place between the plantain skin.
8. Press the plantain to make it flat. Try not to break it up.
9. Place pressed plantain back in skillet & fry till golden brown.
10. Place plantains in a dish layered with napkins so as to drain/soak up the oil.
11. Sprinkle salt to taste.
12. Serves 4

Plantains

Plantains are a member of the banana family. They are a starchy, low in sugar variety that is cooked before serving as it is unsuitable raw. It is used in many savory dishes somewhat like a potato would be used and is very popular in Western Africa and the Caribbean countries. In Jamaica the plantain is simply fried, boiled or added to a soup.

Many people confuse plantains with bananas. Plantains resemble green bananas and are longer than bananas. They have thicker skins and are starchy. They also have natural brown spots and rough areas and ripe plantains may be black in color.

Plátanos Maduros

Plátanos maduros are a delicacy in Jamaica. After removing the skin, the ripened fruit can be sliced (3-4 mm thick) and pan fried in oil until golden brown or according to preference.

Bananas

Bananas are sweet and are eaten as a fruit. The banana is shorter than plantains and has thinner skins. Color is green when not fully ripe, yellow when ripe.

Johnny Cakes "Fried Dumpling"

INGREDIENTS :
4 cups flour
2 teaspoons baking powder
1.5 teaspoon salt
1/2 cup butter or margarine
1/2 cup cold water
1 cup vegetable oil for frying

METHOD:
1. Sift the flour, baking powder, and salt together into a large mixing bowl. Cut in the butter or margarine until the mixture forms marble-sized dough balls. Add the water 1 teaspoon at a time, just enough to bring the dough together with a firm consistency.

2. Heat oil in a heavy bottomed frying pot over medium-low heat until hot

3. Break off pieces and Form the dough into slightly flattened biscuits, about 2 inches across. On a lightly floured surface, knead the dough well, for about five minutes.

4. Fry the Johnny Cakes, so they are not crowded, in the hot oil only until they become golden—(Approx about 2- 3 minutes)

5. Remove the Johnny cakes with and drain on a paper towels to absorb the extra vegetable oil.

6. Johnny cakes are usually served for breakfast with Bully Beef or Ackees. (Serves 6)

Journey Cakes

Also called "Journey Cakes" because you can carry them along on your journey, are actually fried or baked breads. They're a favorite accompaniment to salt fish. It is very similar to hushpuppies.

Native Americans and they were cooking with ground corn "maize". They roasted their corn and ground it into meal to make cakes, breads, and porridges. Cornbread was discovered by Europeans during the exploration of the "New World" and incorporated into their recipes.

Johnny Cakes became a staple of the American cuisine, the American Army as "Hard Tack" a corn biscuit which could be made in different sizes and forms.

Eventually with exploration the Johnny Cake found its way to the West Indies and Australia. It truly has lived up to its name as "Journey Cake"!

Roti (This dish has its roots from India)

INGREDIENTS :
1 cup wheat flour (preferably from an Indian store)
2 tbsp. oil
Salt and enough water to make dough

METHOD:
1. Knead the wheat flour, salt and water to make dough.
2. Let the dough stand for half hour.
3. Take small portions, knead again, dust with flour and roll out into a round shape.
4. Cook in (flat) griddle with a little oil (flip on both sides)
5. You can add many things to the dough and serve with Curry Goat.

Boiled Yams

INGREDIENTS :
3 lbs. Yams
Teaspoon Salt or a small piece Salt fish (cod fish)

METHOD:
1. Put gloves on your hands as touching raw yams will irritate the skin and cause it to itch. If you do not have gloves rub oil on your hands.
2. Boil water in pot on a high fire.
3. Peel the skin off the yam. The peel should be approximately ¼ inch
4. Cut yams in small serving portions
5. Rinse the pieces in cold water.
6. Place the salt or salt fish in the boiling water
7. Add the pieces of yam
8. Cook for approximately 32 minutes until tender
9. Serve warm

Jamaican Carrot Cake

INGREDIENTS :
3 cups of shredded uncooked carrots
4 beaten eggs
1 3/4 pounds brown sugar
2 1/2 cups flour
1 1/2 cup oil
1 teaspoon vanilla
1 1/2 cinnamon
3/4 nutmeg
1/2 teaspoon mixed spice
1 teaspoon baking soda
1/2 teaspoon salt

METHOD:
1. Combine carrot and sugar and mix
2. Add beaten egg, then oil and vanilla and mix well
3. Combine and sift together the flour, cinnamon, spices, nutmeg, mixed spice, baking soda and salt
4. Slowly add the dry ingredients to the wet mixture
5. Pour into greased baking container
6. Bake for 40 minutes at 350F

Bammy

Traditional Jamaican deep-fried cassava flatbread. A fried (or toasted) cake made from flour or meal produced from the cassava, a tuber also known as manioc or yucca. The round cakes are prepared by soaking the dough in coconut milk or water and frying. Bammy is a popular accompaniment to a number of foods, especially fish.

Breadfruit

Breadfruit was also introduced to Jamaica from its native Tahiti in 1793 by the infamous Captain Bligh. Breadfruits are not edible until they are cooked, and they can be used in place of any starchy vegetable, rice, or pasta. Breadfruit is picked and eaten before it ripens and is typically served like squash—baked, grilled, fried, boiled, or roasted after being stuffed with meat.

Jamaican Lemonade

2 oz. Brown Sugar, 16 oz. Water, Ice Cubes

Mix Brown Sugar in a sixteen ounce glass of water until dissolved, add Ice. Squeeze ½ of a lime in this sugar and water solution. Try: ½ of lemon to some sugar cane juice.

Sorrel—Christmas Drink

INGREDIENTS:
1 Pound of Sorrel, 2-4 ounces of Ginger, 2 quarts of water, sugar, Pimento grains 8-12

METHOD:
1. Wash sorrel thoroughly, using the fingers to lift it from the water.
2. Put into stainless steel container.
3. Scrape and wash ginger. Grate and add to the sorrel. Add pimento grains.
4. Boil water and pour over sorrel.
5. Allow to stand 4-6 hours. Strain.
6. Sweeten to taste and add rum to taste.
7. Add optional wine.
8. Serve with ice cubes.

Jamaican Ginger Beer - Easy Recipe

Ingredients:
1 pound of Ginger root, 3 quarts of Water, 2/3 cup Brown Sugar,
3 Lemon or limes juiced

Method
1. Chop the ginger and place the chopped ginger in 3 cups of the
water and 2/3 cup sugar in a blender and puree well. Let set
overnight to extract the entire flavor.
2. Strain the liquid through a fine-meshed sieve and pour into a
pitcher. Add 2 quarts of water and stir in the lemon or lime juice and
additional sugar to taste.
3. Chill well before serving. Makes about 2 quarts.

About the Author

Diane Zimmermann is the oldest of three children who grew up in Staten Island NY. My family is rich in culture, history and adventure which fired my imagination and stirred in me to get out in the world and experience it for myself and to get a good college education and be all that I could be in the Lord Jesus Christ. Thank you God, for hearing a small child's prayers in the dark of night and fulfilling her hopes and dreams!

I have had the privilege in 1971 to visit Europe with my dad's brother Rudy and stay at castle Mondsee with Countess Almedia, and to travel Around-the-World by ship in 1975 with World Campus Afloat. I obtained my Sociology and Masters Degree in Elementary Education from SUNY New Paltz NY, Masters in Library Science from University at Albany, NY, and a Ministers Degree from Church of Living Water, Newark, DE.

I have three wonderful and talented children Jonathan Mandia an Education student, Ensign Jeremy Mandia a Medical student in the US Navy, and Jessica Mandia a Fine Arts Photographer/Art Historian student. My husband Rennie is President of Instrument Services and has three talented sons, Rene is the Vice President and Training Manager for the Bank of New York Mellon, Marc is the Vice President and Chief Financial Officer for American Physicians Service Group, Inc. and Joshua a Computer IT for Cisco Systems. We have five beautiful grandchildren. Rene and Lana have three boys, our twins Reed & Reece, and Ryan who live in Huston Texas. Marc and Ashley have a boy and a girl Zachery and Kaitlyn who live in Austin Texas.

I am proud of my family and knowing something about their lives describes the positive impact they had on me. My mother's parents immigrated to America from Italy in 1903 taking passage in the bottom of the ships. My Grandmother Gilda Zona Boschetto was a great woman of God and impacted my life in many ways. She took me to church, was faithful in supporting missions around the world and who helped me develop in the Lord.

A great storyteller in her own right, she would tell me about her life in Piedmont Italy, Napoleon and her family's stories, which I recorded. She fired my imagination and my love to learn and write about history and cultures of the world. Her grandfather had a sign over their home that said "Casa de Levine" and they were Sephardic Jews. Gilda the youngest of 4 was orphaned at age 12, came to America at age 16, by ship as steerage passenger, and married Quinto Boschetto, in 1903 became a seamstress and in 1911, survived the Triangle Shirtwaist Factory fire in NYC. In 1912 her infant son died to Influenza and in 1916, 11 year old Mario died due to a cerebral hemorrhage on his birthday. She raised Dante and my mother Gloria on Staten Island.

My grandfather Quinto Boschetto was Chef de Cuisine for the great Hotels in NYC. He enlisted in the Army in WWI and the Merchant Marine during WWII. His ship was torpedoed by a German U-boat and he was picked up in the icy Atlantic by the British. He and traveled all around the world, brang home stories of his travels and gifts from Japan. My mother Gloria Percoco was a talented artist, gifted pianist and a wonderful mother and she filled our home with her music, art and love for my sister Gloria and my brother Joseph and me.

My dad Joseph Percoco impacted my life in so many ways. He was a survivor of infantile paralysis and was blind as a child because of his illness. His mother Josephine would sit him in the sunshine and nurtured him back to health. His father Felix also an immigrant became a salesman who raised 10 children in Little Italy in Manhattan during the Depression and provided for them during hard times.

I remember my dad was a Good Humor Ice cream man and would come with home with his truck and white uniform and he could tell you the name of every flavor of ice cream they had. His brother Rudy (who later married Countess Michelin Almeida a direct descendant of Macmillan Joseph 1st king of Bavaria) and my dad traveled around the US and Canada with Mirth Shows, "The All-American Indian Village" education program in the 1960's. Our headliner was Chief John Big Tree, who poised for the Indian Head Nickel, designed by James Earl Fraser in 1913. Later my dad became the Food and beverage manager of the Chrysler Building in NYC, and owner of the Piccadilly Circus Restaurant on SI with my mother.

Look for my other books:
Book of Wisdom, Proverbs for a Hungry Soul: Finding God's plan for our life.
Zona's Quest: About my grandmother's Italian heritage, family and their stories.
The All-America Indian Village: about my dad's adventures and his stories.
The Count and Countess of Mondsee Austria: about my Rudy and the Countesses family.

I believe that everyone needs to tell a good story and pass on the oral traditions of their culture.

God bless,
Rev Dr. Diane L. Zimmerman